CHEAP BASTARD'S® SERIES

THE CHEAP BASTARD'S® GUIDE TO

Las Vegas

Secrets of Living the Good Life—For Less!

First Edition

Shaena **Engle**

Guilford, Connecticut
An imprint of Globe Pequot Press

All the information in this guidebook is subject to change. We recommend that you call ahead to obtain current information before traveling.

To buy books in quantity for corporate use or incentives, call **(800) 962–0973** or e-mail **premiums@GlobePequot.com**.

Text design by Sheryl P. Kober

Library of Congress Cataloging-in-Publication Data is available on file.
ISBN 978-0-7627-6002-2

Printed in the United States of America
10 9 8 7 6 5 4 3 2 1

To the fabulous men.
Thanks Dad for your all of your helpful advice.
Thanks to my nephew Wyatt
for hours of free entertainment and laughter.
And of course, thanks to Matt, for never being cheap
with his love and support.

CONTENTS

ACKNOWLEDGMENTS

Here's the part where I need to thank everyone who put in much more than their two cents of help. None were cheap or stingy with their valuable time and input.

Thanks to Amy Lyons, Kevin Sirois, Lynn Zelem, and everyone at Globe Pequot Press. Thanks to my agent, Julie A. Hill, for help getting the gig and making sure everything ran smoothly.

Thanks to everyone in Las Vegas, Ernesto Aespinosar, Chef Jin Caldwell, Alicia Malone and everyone from the Las Vegas Convention and Visitors Authority, Joni Moss, Emily Woffard at R&R Partners, the folks at Kirvin Doak and Langdon Flynn, and all the PR folks who helped me locate information. Thanks also to all the folks at the many wedding chapels, restaurants, shows, and other venues who took the time to speak with me and provide so much information. And thanks to the PR folks at Wynn and Venetian who always take care of me when I work on numerous other articles and projects in Sin City.

Thanks to my sidekicks who helped along the way, sitting through tons of dinners and events. They include Sheila Afnan Mann (my smart and generous friend and shopping, eating, and show-watching partner in Sin City), Paul McCreesh and Chris Lucas, Nicole Okudaira, Dalbert Buitrago, Sachi Wadsworth, poker mavens Gina and Tom Hershey, and my mom, Anne Engle. Thanks also to Todd Shea, Raymond Swift, Mario Medelin, John Buck, and magician extraordinaire Michael Vincent. Thanks to Dr. Daniel Stone and Preston Hillier for keeping me healthy after so many big Vegas meals.

INTRODUCTION

In the '70s, Las Vegas was the land of comps and cash payouts, of free drinks and entertainment, of endless bargain buffets and cheap eats galore. It was a city that lavished hospitality on the rich and lured the rest of us with the promise of inexpensive meals, rooms, and shows with a long-shot fantasy of walking away an instant millionaire.

Vegas was flatlining by the early '80s, so it reinvented itself as an inexplicably family-friendly destination. Once the casinos figured out that kids, liquor, and slots don't mix and business kept declining, a new salacious campaign launched to make Sin City the kind of place you didn't even tell your spouse you were visiting (and you refused to talk about any details when you got home).

Long known as the home of cheap and cheesy kitsch, casino companies worked hard during the '80s and '90s to shed Vegas's bargain image, remodeling themed hotels into luxury vacation resorts and opening one celebrity chef gourmet restaurant after another. Nightclubs demanding hundreds of dollars for a bottle of Ketel One popped up in every major casino, while hotels turned their pools into dayclubs that charged the equivalent of a mortgage payment just to sit in a cabana and get some shade.

Just when it looked like Britney Spears, championship poker, and $400-a-night-suites were going to become the norm, the economy took a nosedive. The upside of the current economy may be that what happens in Vegas is that you might actually be able to afford to stay in Vegas.

Things are noticeably quieter on the Strip, and casinos usually known to boast excess are dropping prices to cope with the bad economy that has hit Sin City particularly hard.

A return to the mind-set that got our parents hooked on this neon desert in the '60s and '70s is back. Get folks here on the cheap, keep them fed and cocktailed for free, and they won't notice they're blowing their now-diminished life savings on the slot machines.

Today, gaming revenue, visitation, and occupancy rates are all in a free fall.

While that's bad news overall for the casino industry, there's a bit of good news in there for all budget-conscious consumers (aka cheap bastards). Those spiraling numbers are dragging down prices of rooms, food, and shows.

Today you're likely to find deals such as prix fixe multicourse menus where your total bill costs what you would have tipped when times were better; $19 room rates (okay, not on the Strip, but Strip-adjacent in beautiful downtown Sin City); and dining, player card, and entertainment credits just for staying in certain hotels.

The fact is that Las Vegas needs visitors, rather badly, as a matter of its own survival. Consequently, the past months have seen a proliferation of affordable hotel rates as well as a preponderance of meal deals and spa, golf, and booze comp packages the likes of which haven't been seen since the Clinton administration.

As a travel and food writer I am used to getting the royal treatment during press trips to Las Vegas. I usually stay at the big resorts, eat at the latest restaurants, and drop in at the trendy bars and lounges. Of course, I don't pay for any of it.

Doing research for this book I paid my own way for most things, and boy was I shocked. Who in this economy can afford the high-end Strip hotel and restaurant prices? When I actually had to spend my own meager paycheck on travel and food, you can bet I couldn't afford to slumber at the Bellagio.

I learned that Las Vegas has plenty of inexpensive fun things to do and see without stinging financial stakes. Now that prices have fallen and there are deals to find, you really can have fun in Lost Wages, even when your budget is as tight as the casino slots.

This book features things that are totally free, free with a catch (a condition or with some sort of strings attached), and just plain cheap. I hope you find this book useful and that it uncovers new, interesting, and inexpensive things to occupy your time in the city that is designed to part you from your money.

Historical Timeline

Las Vegas moved from a simple settlement to today's megaresort destination in 100 years. Here's how:

1829: Discovered by Spanish explorers.

1855: First settled by Mormons.

1905: Town of Las Vegas established by land auction.

1911: The city of Las Vegas is incorporated.

1931: Gambling legalized in Nevada.

1941: El Rancho Vegas opens on the Strip. El Cortez Hotel opens downtown.

1942: Last Frontier Hotel opens.

1946: Gangster Bugsy Siegel opens Flamingo Hotel.

1966: Howard Hughes arrives to live at Desert Inn.

1975: Nevada gaming revenues crack $1 billion mark.

1979: Liberace Museum opens.

1989: Mirage opens Nov. 22, with 3,039 rooms.

1990: Excalibur opens June 19, then the world's largest resort hotel, with 4,032 rooms.

1993: Money won by Nevada casinos tops the $6 billion mark. MGM Grand Hotel and Theme Park opens, with 5,005 rooms and a 171,500-square-foot casino, making it the largest resort hotel-casino in the world.

1994: Downtown Fremont Street is permanently closed to auto traffic. Hard Rock Hotel opens. $25 million monorail begins running between MGM Grand and Bally's on June 14. The $70 million Fremont Street Experience opens in December.

1995: Las Vegas reports 29 million visitors for the year. Wayne Newton celebrates his 25,000th Las Vegas performance. Siegfried and Roy celebrate their 15,000th Las Vegas performance.

1996: Opening of Stratosphere Tower, tallest free-standing observation tower in the United States and the tallest structure west of the Mississippi River. 29.6 million people visit Las Vegas, and Clark County population hits 1.1 million.

1997: New York New York Hotel Casino opens on the Las Vegas Strip on Jan. 3. More than 100,000 people a day visit the new resort during its first days in operation.

1998: Bellagio, billed as the most expensive hotel in the world ($1.7 billion), opens Oct. 15. The hotel bars people younger than 18 who are not registered guests. Number of visitors to Las Vegas that year tops 30 million.

2002: Neonopolis entertainment center opens downtown.

2003: The Fashion Show mall completes a $1 billion expansion.

2004: The Las Vegas Monorail, a $654 million mass transit system, opens.

2005: Wynn Las Vegas, the destination's newest megaresort, opens Apr. 28. At $2.7 billion, the resort becomes the most expensive hotel and casino in the world. Las Vegas celebrates its 100th birthday on May 15. The destination's tagline, "What happens in Vegas stays in Vegas" firmly cements itself into the American lexicon. MGM Mirage announces Project CityCenter, an "urban metropolis" with 4,000 hotel rooms and 1,650 condominium units. Project CityCenter will cost nearly $5 billion, making it the largest privately funded project in the United States.

2006: Nevada celebrates 75 years of legalized gaming.

2007: Fremont East Entertainment District Improvement Project celebrates its groundbreaking to revitalize downtown. Tropicana Resort & Casino celebrates 50 years on the Las Vegas Strip. The Stardust Hotel & Casino is imploded. The Las Vegas Springs Preserve opens to the public. This 180-acre cultural and historic attraction features museums, galleries, and more. Town Square Las Vegas, a new retail, dining, and entertainment project, opens on South Las Vegas Boulevard.

2008: The Palazzo celebrates its grand opening. Golden Nugget completes a $60 million expansion including adding convention space and a new nightclub. Encore Las Vegas opens in December.

2009: Las Vegas Convention Center Celebrates 50th Anniversary on April 12. Dubai World and MGM Mirage open the 16.5-billion-square-foot City Center complex, housing Vdara, Crystals, Aria, and Mandarin Oriental. With a total cost of $11 billion, City Center is the largest privately financed development in the United States.

2010: After a two year hiatus, Celine Dion announces that she will return to Las Vegas in a new show at Caesars Palace.

Entertainment in Las Vegas

THEATER:
FREE & NEXT TO NOTHING SHOWS

"First of all, I choose the great [roles],
and if none of these come,
I choose the mediocre ones,
and if they don't come,
I choose the ones that pay the rent."
—MICHAEL CAINE

Over the past few years, theater went through a metamorphosis in Las Vegas. Since the mid '90s, Sin City has been a port of call for well-known Broadway musicals including the *Phantom of the Opera*, *Jersey Boys*, *Mamma Mia*, *Hairspray*, and *The Lion King*. In most cases, these musicals are diet versions of the original Broadway productions, slimmed down to fit two shows per night and turn a maximum profit.

Just like everything else in Vegas, theater is all about the eye candy. In terms of sheer special effects firepower, Vegas blows Broadway away. Cirque de Soleil, with its eight productions on the Strip, dishes out enough high-tech razzle-dazzle to drop the jaw of even the most jaded theatergoer. But getting your Cirque on, and just about any other major show here, stuns wallets to the tune of at least $100. If you know where to go, you can find some shows on the cheap.

JUST **PLAIN** FREE

[handwritten note: Show Not showing everyday Has cheesecake Factory]

✓ Fall of Atlantis Fountain Show
3570 Las Vegas Blvd. South
(866) 227-5938
www.caesarspalace.com

Soap opera drama can be found at the Forum Shops in the Fall of Atlantis Show, where lifelike animatronic figures battle it out to see who will rule Atlantis. A huge-winged beast eventually appears and the mythical city is consumed by fire and flooding water. Behind the fountain lies a cool 50,000-gallon saltwater aquarium with more than 100 species of fish and plants.

✓ Festival Fountain Show
3570 Las Vegas Blvd. South
(866) 227-5938
www.caesarspalace.com

The Festival Fountain Show is a technological spectacle complete with animated statues of Roman gods and a plotline that could rival any Strip show.

Every hour on the hour, seven days a week, the white marble statue of Bacchus comes to life and welcomes visitors to the mall by planning a party. He awakens fellow statues Apollo and Plutus for help. Apollo plays his lute and Plutus decorates the fountain with colored lighting effects in water. Venus also joins in. The rotunda is illuminated with lasers, theatrical lighting, and projections of mythological images. The best part is the price—free!

Fountains at Bellagio

3600 Las Vegas Blvd. South
(702) 693-7111
www.bellagio.com

If you're visiting Bellagio at night, make sure to see the best free show in Vegas—the Bellagio Water Fountains. Here you can enjoy giant spouts shooting water hundreds of feet in the air in the middle of the desert, dancing, swirling, and swaying to music ranging from Broadway tunes to Sinatra to symphonic, all on Steve Wynn's dime. If you sit here long enough you can enjoy two shows for the price of one and yet still have paid exactly nothing. Shows are every half hour starting early afternoon, and every 15 minutes from 7 p.m. to midnight.

Fremont Street Experience

425 Fremont St.
(702) 678-5600
www.vegasexperience.com

After the Bellagio fountains, the Glitter Gulch Lights on Fremont Street are the next best free show. If you're feeling like Nicholas Cage in *Leaving Las Vegas* and the "glamorous acrobatic show/celebrity chef restaurant" Vegas isn't quite right for your partying mood, then it's time to visit the tiny old downtown area of the city. Vegas's effort to spruce up downtown is the four-block stretch of Fremont Street, a pedestrian-only zone that's covered with a video screen with 12.5 million lights and a 500,000-watt sound system. Yes, it's a bit like the fireworks show at Disneyland on crack—but much louder and brighter, and surrounded by all sorts of real life cartoon characters known as Las Vegas locals. Every night from 8 p.m. to midnight an hourly sound and light extravaganza entertains the crowds below.

Masquerade in the Sky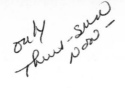

Rio Hotel
3700 West Flamingo Rd.
(866) 746-7671
www.riolasvegas.com

At the Rio Hotel, the magical experience of "Masquerade in the Sky" is not created on a stage or screen but literally high overhead. This one-of-a-kind celebration of Carnival in Rio and Mardi Gras features pulsating music, scantily clad performers, and parade floats that circle high above the casino floor below.

Sirens of TI

2200 Las Vegas Blvd. South
(702) 894-7111
www.treasureisland.com

Outside of TI (Treasure Island), "The Sirens of TI," a techno-pulsating spectacular of high seas drama comes to life nightly in the water-filled lagoon. The Sirens (in Greek mythology, a group of scantily clad well-endowed goddesses—or maybe that's just in Las Vegas) lure a shipload of shirtless six-pack-abbed mariners to their vessel in the show at 6, 8, and 10 p.m. nightly, complete with blasting music, choreography, and lots of lights. The plot is absurd, but it's also free and fun.

Wynn Lake of Dreams

Wynn Hotel
3131 Las Vegas Blvd. South
(877) 321-9966
www.wynnlasvegas.com

The Catch The show can be watched only if you are dining in the Daniel Boulud Brasserie, the Steakhouse, or the Parasol or Chanel bars.

Twice an hour, this man-made lake lights up with a variety of colors to classic tunes and an extravaganza of psychedelic hologram images projected on the wall waterfall, while a huge frog and puppets also appear. If you want to watch but can't afford the pricy drinks and grub, nab a coveted spot on the small viewing platform set above these venues on the casino level.

SCORING **CHEAP** DISCOUNT **TICKETS**

Many shows can no longer afford to let unsold seats simply go empty—or free to casino high rollers. Enter the two major discount companies, **All Access Entertainment** and **Tix4Tonight**, ticket heaven for theater buffs. These two venues average discounts of one-third off of Ticketmaster's price for the most popular shows and half off for the less popular ones.

All Access Entertainment
Aztec Inn Casino
2200 Las Vegas Blvd. South

Circus Circus
2880 Las Vegas Blvd. South
Two kiosks located here

Fashion Mall Food Court
3200 Las Vegas Blvd. South

Palace Station
2411 West Sahara Ave.

Slots-O-Fun
2890 Las Vegas Blvd. South

South Point Hotel
9777 Las Vegas Blvd. South

Tahiti Village
7200 Las Vegas Blvd. South

Tuscany Suites
255 East Flamingo Rd.

All Access offers eight box office locations around the Strip, all selling discount general admission and VIP tickets. Shows are listed at 9:30 a.m. and box offices open at 10 a.m. daily.

Tix4Tonight
Fashion Show Mall in front of Neiman Marcus
3200 Las Vegas Blvd. South

Hawaiian Marketplace, 3743 Las Vegas Blvd. South

Bill's Gambling Hall, 3595 Las Vegas Blvd. South

Showcase Mall, 3785 South Las Vegas Blvd.

Four Queens Hotel, 202 Fremont St.

Tix4Tonight discounts slightly more on average than All Access. Their per-ticket service fee also tends to run less, but they offer fewer locations than their competitor. Shows are listed at 9:30 a.m. and box offices open at 10 a.m. daily.

Best of Vegas
www.bestofvegas.com

Before you hop on a plane or get behind the wheel and head to the desert, check the Best of Vegas Web site to compare prices on shows prior to arriving on the Strip. By buying through this Web site, you can not only score discounted tickets but also receive free seat upgrades.

ALWAYS **CHEAP:** OFF-STRIP **THEATER**

Las Vegas Little Theatre
3920 Schiff Dr.
(702) 362-7996
http://lvlt.org
$22 for main stage performances, $12 for Blackbox performances

This small 48-seat venue is Las Vegas's oldest community theater. Founded in 1978, it offers classic critically acclaimed plays performed by amateur actors for amateur prices, in two separate theaters. The smaller Blackbox Theater performances are even cheaper than the main stage plays.

Movies Made in Las Vegas

You can hardly blame filmmakers for being endlessly fascinated with Las Vegas as a setting for their movies. Elvis Presley and Ann-Margret swiveling across the silver screen in *Viva Las Vegas*. Flying Elvises dropping from the sky onto the glitzy neon Strip in *Honeymoon in Vegas*. Robert De Niro and Sharon Stone capturing the city's sordid romance with the mob in *Casino*. Hollywood loves doing Vegas.

The movie industry's romance with this city dates from the 1940s. The city's glamour, dynamic growth, and seedy past provide a wealth of story ideas and locales.

Here are some titles to put you in the mood for more:

Las Vegas Nights (1941)
Helldorado (1946)
The Las Vegas Story (1952)
Meet Me in Las Vegas
   (1956)
Amazing Colossal Man
   (1957)
The Joker Is Wild (1957)
Ocean's Eleven (1960)
Viva Las Vegas (1964)
Diamonds Are Forever
   (1971)

The Night Stalker (1971)
The Godfather (1972)
The Gambler (1974)
One From the Heart (1982)
Corvette Summer (1978)
Electric Horseman (1979)
Melvin and Howard (1980)
Thief (1981)
Things Are Tough All Over
   (1982)
Oh God, You Devil (1984)
Starman (1984)

Rainbow Community Youth Theatre

Reed Whipple Cultural Center
821 Las Vegas Blvd. North
(702) 229-6553
www.rainbowcompany.org
Shows at 2 and 7 p.m.
$7 for adults, $5 for teens and seniors

The stars are young (ages 10 to 18) but the talent is pure Vegas. Forty tweens and teens perform classics such as *Joseph and the Amazing Technicolor Dreamcoat* and *The Orphan Train* at this small community theater.

Lost in America (1985)
Prizzi's Honor (1985)
Rocky IV (1985)
Midnight Run (1988)
Rain Man (1988)
Bugsy (1991)
Honey, I Blew Up the Kid (1993)
Honeymoon in Vegas (1993)
Indecent Proposal (1993)
Casino (1995)
Leaving Las Vegas (1995)
Showgirls (1995)
Mars Attacks! (1996)
Vegas Vacation (1997)
Con Air (1997)
Fools Rush In (1997)
Austin Powers: International Man of Mystery (1997)

Fear and Loathing in Las Vegas (1998)
Lethal Weapon 4 (1998)
Pay it Forward (2000)
Rush Hour 2 (2001)
Ocean's Eleven (2001)
America's Sweethearts (2001)
The Cooler (2003)
Dodgeball: A True Underdog Story (2004)
Miss Congeniality 2: Armed and Fabulous (2005)
Lucky You (2005)
Rocky Balboa (2006)
Ocean's Thirteen (2007)
Knocked Up (2007)
21 (2008)
What Happens in Vegas (2008)
The Hangover (2009)

Theatre in the Valley

Performances at City of Henderson Convention Center
200 South Water St., Henderson
(702) 558-7275
www.theatreinthevalley.org
Adults $12, seniors and students $10

This roaming theater company (performance venues vary, so check their Web site) produces three plays per year, including classics such as *Who's Afraid of Virginia Woolf?* and *Ten Little Indians*. Local Vegas thespians show their stuff off the Strip, so performances may not be stellar but you can get a ticket for a song.

MUSIC:
FOR A SONG

"The music business is a cruel and shallow money trench, a long plastic hallway where thieves and pimps run free, and good men die like dogs. There's also a negative side."

—HUNTER S. THOMPSON

Sin City is the place where "lounge" was raised to high art and practiced to its mellow sexy perfection by Frank, Dino, and Sammy. Vegas still swings today, but prices to see big name acts are steep. Wayne Newton, Barry Manilow, Cher, and Elton John tap into baby boomers' memories and wallets, and impersonators who've spent their lives mimicking the motions and music of Madonna and Prince prevail. There is still a good range of free and affordable live acts if you know where to go.

FREE (**AND** ALMOST **FREE**) LOUNGES

The Access Showroom
Aliante Casino
7300 Aliante Pkwy.
(702) 692-7777
www.alientecasinohotel.com
Saturday night: Caliante Noche Latina, $5 cover; Thursday night: Rat Pack Thursdays, $5 cover

Head to the Access Showroom, where you can listen to music from Caliante Noche Latina on Saturday, a five-man-one-woman Latin group, to Rat Pack Thursdays, where you can listen to renditions of the swinging sounds of Frank, Dean, and Sammy. Get your groove on or just chill out in one of the 650 bar seats.

Artisan Hotel Lounge
Artisan Hotel
1501 West Sahara Ave.
(702) 214-4000
www.artisanhotel.com
No Cover

Join the Hollywood hipsters at this ultra chic lounge where live bands play on Thursday nights and DJ McKenzie spins house music and top 40 hits on weekends.

Back Alley Bar

Stratosphere
2000 Las Vegas Blvd. South
(702) 383-4777
www.stratospherehotel.com
No Cover

The Catch If you are going to the Stratosphere to take on the rides, save the drink till after your thrills. Your stomach and the folks below will thank you.

Visit the Back Alley Bar on weekends for live music by local bands and draft beers served up by Daisy Duke–clad servers.

Bill's Lounge

Bill's Gamblin' Hall and Saloon
3594 Las Vegas Blvd. South
(702) 737-2100
www.billslasvegas.com
No Cover

Spend an hour with the King, Peter "Big Elvis" Vallee, as he performs rock, country, gospel, and R&B classics spanning six decades of music. Songs and sideburns from this super-sized entertainer are free, with three shows every weekday, Mon through Fri, at 3, 5, and 6:30 p.m.

Cabo Lounge and Club Tequila

Fiesta Rancho
2400 North Rancho Dr.
(702) 631-7000
www.fiestarancholasvegas.com

The Catch Club Tequila enforces a $5 cover for men

Remember spring break in Cabo drinking tequila? Well, this is nothing like that. The Cabo Lounge offers generic rock bands playing '70s, '80s, and '90s hits to an older local crowd, and DJs at Club Tequila spin dance hits for a $5 cover.

Caramel Lounge

Bellagio
3600 Las Vegas Blvd. South
(702) 693-7111
www.lightgroup.com
No Cover

Everything about Caramel is yummy, from the warm caramel-colored couches to the giant glass sculptures. What's really tasty is the price—it doesn't cost anything to enjoy the elegant atmosphere, listen to lounge music, mingle with the beautiful people, or take a break from the constant ringing of the slots at this sweet spot.

Carnival Court
Harrah's
3475 Las Vegas Blvd. South
(702) 369-5000
www.harrahs.com
No Cover

If you just can't decide among gambling, flirting with strangers, dancing, or drinking the day or night away, check out Carnival Court where you can do it all in one place. Sip on a cocktail while watching the free show put on by cute flair bartenders or gamble at the blackjack tables while listening to the daily live bands on stage.

Cleopatra's Barge
Caesars Palace
3570 Las Vegas Blvd. South
(866) 227-5938
www.caesarspalace.com
No Cover

The Catch Entrance is free but drinks can be pricey and the crowd is often made up of older (think 40+) clientele.

This old-school floating Egyptian lounge literally rocks (it's on the water) with live bands performing covers of dance songs. Walk the "moat" and groove to hits pre-1985.

The Club and Pin-Ups Lounge
Cannery Casino
2121 East Craig Rd.
(703) 507-5700
www.cannerycasinos.com
Prices vary, free and up

Located in the center of the casino area, Pin-Ups Lounge offers live music nightly for mostly locals, while the Club, an indoor/outdoor space, houses performers ranging from tribute bands (Neil Diamond, Elvis, the Beatles, and the Rolling Stones) to professional singers (O'Jays, Merle Haggard).

Club Madrid
Sunset Station
1301 West Sunset Rd.
(702) 547-7777
www.stationcasinos.com
Prices vary, free and up

This 500-seat lounge features free live music nights with local bands playing Motown, metal, classic rock, and country. It also features headliners that require admission fees, so check the calendar for event listings.

Dixie's Dam Bar
Hooters
115 East Tropicana Blvd.
(702) 617-7777
www.hooterscasinohotel.com
No Cover

Located inside Hooters, the only location of the nationwide franchise where the waitresses aren't overdressed, this casual rock 'n' roll bar offers DJs spinning the latest sounds and a keg service—$200 for 60 12-ounce beers—but the music is free. Views of the leather halter top and fringe short-shorts clad servers are also no charge.

Eyecandy Sound Lounge
Mandalay Bay
3950 Las Vegas Blvd. South
(702) 632-7777
www.mandalaybay.com
No Cover

In the middle of all the casino action at Mandalay Bay sits Eyecandy, a high-tech nightlife experience. This large open space has pulsating colored lighting, a sleek teardrop-shaped bar, dance floor, and DJs spinning hits nightly. The best features are the gauze-curtained "pod tables" featuring iPad-like touch screens, where you can communicate and flirt with other tables.

4949 Lounge
Santa Fe Station
4949 North Rancho Dr.
(702) 658-4900
www.stationcasinos.com
No Cover

This new circular lounge features loads of free stuff. The Spazmatics perform live on Friday when all guests can get a free Red Bull and vodka. Prize drawings for free stuff including movie tickets, bowling, and drinks are nightly. Go Friday night between 9 and 10 p.m. and get a free drink!

Gold Coast Showroom Lounge
Gold Coast
4000 West Flamingo Rd.
(702) 367-7111
www.goldcoastcasino.com
No Cover

When Society of Seven isn't occupying the Showroom Lounge, a variety of free live music including jazz, rock, Latin, and disco can be found day and night at this local fave, conveniently located adjacent to the Rio.

Gold Diggers
Golden Nugget
129 Fremont St.
(702) 385-7111
www.goldennugget.com
No Cover

Pass by the 61-pound golden nugget to the free jewel at this renowned casino—the free music and view of the nightly neon light show on Fremont Street—at Gold Diggers. DJs spin fave hits from the '70s up to get your groove on.

Gonzalez Y Gonzalez
New York New York
3790 Las Vegas Blvd. South
(866) 805-4365
www.nynyhotelcasino.com
No Cover

Weekend nights are *muy caliente* at Dulce Latin Night at Gonzalez Y Gonzalez, where couples can tango, salsa, and shimmy to sounds in Español and electronica.

I-Bar
Rio
3700 West Flamingo Rd.
(866) 746-7671
www.riolasvegas.com
No Cover

This ultra hip techno savvy lounge offers visitors a chance to go virtual. Tables include touch screens allowing guests to flirt with other tables, create signature cocktails, play interactive games, and take a virtual walk down the Strip while enjoying house and pop music.

Karaoke Club
Imperial Palace
3535 Las Vegas Blvd. South
(702) 731-3311
www.imperialpalace.com
No Cover

Divas and *American Idol* wannabes can be the star of the show at this free Karaoke Club, featuring over 15,000 songs from Alabama to ZZ Top. For a small fee, you can memorialize your performance on a DVD to view when you are sober.

Kixx Lounge
Boulder Station
4111 Boulder Hwy.
(702) 432-7777
www.boulderstation.com
No Cover

This 24-hour lounge offers video poker, drinks, and a chance for you to be the star of the show at their weekend "Shooting Stars" karaoke nights on Thurs, Fri, and Sat.

Marilyn's Lounge

Eastside Cannery
5222 Boulder Hwy.
(702) 856-5300
www.cannerycasinos.com
No Cover

While the Casablanca Room hosts boxing matches and headline performers such as the Commodores and LeeAnn Rimes with prices for tickets running $40 and up, Marilyn's Lounge offers every kind of live music—from Fab Four tribute bands to R&B to high energy disco—all for free.

Napoleon's Lounge

Paris
3655 Las Vegas Blvd. South
(702) 946-7000
www.parislasvegas.com
No Cover

Whisk over to 19th-century France at Napoleon's Lounge, where you can sample more than 100 champagnes and sparkling wines at this *tres* Paris bar which also features nightly live jazz and dueling pianists.

Naughty Ladies Saloon

Arizona Charlie's Decatur
740 South Decatur Blvd.
(702) 258-5111
www.arizonacharlies.com
No Cover

Baby boomers can dance the night away to their favorite hits from the '50s and '60s each Tuesday night when the Bee-Bop Brothers spin the oldies, while young'uns can enjoy live bands on weekend nights.

Oasis Lounge

Sam's Town Live
5111 Boulder Hwy.
(702) 456-7777
www.samstownlv.com

Listen live to talk show host Dennis Bono interview guests and sing standards in the afternoon and come back in the evening to hear free jazz every Friday night.

Ovation Lounge and Quinn's Irish Pub
Green Valley Ranch
2300 Paseo Verde Pkwy.
(702) 617-7777
www.greenvalleyranchresort.com
No Cover

After a day of shopping at the adjoining District, fashionistas can show off their wares at the modern and intimate Ovation Lounge, where good local bands provide some of the Strip's best free casino music. The more casual and energetic Quinn's Irish Pub offers brews and Irish music and modern rock.

Primm Valley Piano Bar
Terrible's Casino
31900 Las Vegas Blvd. South
(702) 386-7867
www.terriblescasinos.com
No Cover

Chill out to the soulful serenades of various local jazz groups at this small intimate piano bar. Sit back and sip libations to the tunes of some of the area's most talented pianists.

Shimmer Showroom
Hilton
3000 Paradise Rd.
(702) 732-5755
www.lvhilton.com

The Catch One drink minimum.

Sin City Heat, a singing, dancing, and gyrating rock group, performs choreographed numbers nightly. There's not much fire to this group's cover songs of the '70s, but for the price of a drink you can keep entertained.

South Padre

Texas Station
2101 Texas Star Lane
(702) 631-1000
www.stationcasinos.com
No Cover

Enjoy a mix of live entertainment from local bands and DJs spinning the latest hits on Friday and Saturday nights, then get your swing on to the smooth sounds of the Jerry Tiffe Band on Sunday afternoon.

V Bar

Venetian
3355 Las Vegas Blvd. South
(702) 414-3200
www.venetian.com
No Cover

This small modern bar is a great alternative to the pricey Tao, offering sophistication and sultry appeal. No need to worry about long entrance lines or expensive cover charges—there aren't any. The low lighting and secluded seating areas make this a good spot for intimate encounters.

BARS, **CLUBS**, AND **RESTAURANTS**

Beauty Bar

517 East Fremont St.
(702) 598-1965
www.beautybar.com
No Cover

DJs and live bands rotate nightly at this cool retro bar designed to resemble a 1950s New Jersey beauty saloon. On Friday night, you can mix music, martinis, and manicures amidst old-school hair dryer sets.

Bootlegger Bistro

7700 Las Vegas Blvd. South
(702) 736-4939
www.bootleggerlasvegas.com
No Cover

This Italian restaurant tucked away a few miles south of the megaresorts is a secret to most out-of-towners. Entertainment is a throwback to the lounge-act days of Louis Prima, with local faves singing standards and torch songs. The Bootlegger is open 24 hours, so order up a dish of spaghetti and meatballs whenever you get a craving for authentic Vegas entertainment and food.

Brendan's Irish Pub

The Orleans
4500 West Tropicana Ave.
(702) 365-7111
www.orleanscasino.com
No Cover

Order up an ale and enjoy the bevy of Irish bands, jazz groups, and Zydeco troops or go with a gaggle of pals to play pool at this authentic pub, where the average drink price is only $4.

Bunkhouse Saloon

124 South 11th St.
(702) 384-4536
www.bunkhouselv.com
No Cover

Locals who tire of searching for great live music on the Strip head to the Bunkhouse Saloon, which is about as far from a casino ultra lounge as you can get. Designed with a cowboy theme, you can play pool or darts, order up some basic grub, and listen to everything from punk to rockabilly to reggae. Frugal barhoppers can enjoy buy-one-get-one-free appetizers and two well drinks for only $5 from 4 to 7 p.m. daily.

Charlie's

5012 Arville St.
(702) 876-1844
www.charlieslasvegas.com
No Cover

This country and western gay bar offers male divas a chance to two-step with Brokeback cowboys under a disco ball. You can find it all here—from drag queen bingo to underwear night. Sunday nights also offer disco music in addition to the weekly country tunes. Free line dancing lessons are offered on Monday and Thursday nights.

Cheyenne Saloon
3103 North Rancho Dr.
(702) 645-4139
www.thecheyennesaloon.com
$5 to $10 cover charge

Way north of the Strip lies this dive bar which features local punk, alternative and rock music. Not for the faint of heart, the drinks are cheap, the music is loud, and the neighborhood is sketchy.

Crown & Anchor British Pub
1350 East Tropicana Ave.
(702) 739-8676
www.crownandanchorlv.com
No Cover

This traditional British pub offers live music on Saturday nights, though most bands aren't from across the pond and rarely sound like the Beatles. The food is worth ordering, with authentic pub items, 24-hour service, and graveyard menu specials. Down $2 drink specials during weekday happy hour from 3 to 6 p.m.

Dino's
1516 Las Vegas Blvd. South
(702) 382-3894
www.dinoslv.com
No Cover

Why max out your credit cards to see Elton, Cher, or Bette when you can watch Danny G do shots of Jagermeister and belt out classics for free? This downtown no-frills dive bar is a hotspot for cheapskates and kitschmongers alike.

Double Down Saloon

4640 Paradise Rd.
(702) 791-5774
www.doubledownsaloon.com
Free

The Catch Shows usually don't start till after midnight so be prepared for a late night.

This faux-seedy dive has lots of Vegas character, including a "you puke, you clean" sign above the bar. Party the night away to live punk and rock music for as long as your legs, liver, and wallet hold out.

Downtown Cocktail Room

111 Las Vegas Blvd. South
(702) 880-3696
www.downtownlv.com
No Cover

This dark, dimly lit, chic bar specializes in serving classic cocktails to local hipsters. The design is romantic, the drinks are retro and the music is provided by Brooklyn-based DJs. Beers from $3 and $5 well drinks and wine offered weekdays from 4 to 8 p.m.

Freakin' Frog

4700 Maryland Pkwy.
(702) 597-3237
www.freakinfrog.com
No Cover

Located across from UNLV, this old-school college pub houses more than 350 beer selections and offers traditional comfort food to go with live jazz music every Tuesday evening. Buy-one-get-one-free beer specials are offered daily from 3 to 7 p.m.

The Griffon

511 Fremont St.
(702) 382-0577
No Cover

You might think you stepped into the movie *Swingers* when visiting this downtown spot, with leather booths, fireplaces, and stiff drinks. Hang with the hipsters and listen to cool sounds spun nightly by local DJs. Daily $3 draft beers and well drinks from 5 to 8 p.m.

Hofbräuhaus
4510 Paradise Rd.
(702) 853-2337
www.hofbrauhauslasvegas.com
No Cover

[handwritten: Fun + Good food / Although SALTY Food / About $100 couple with Drinks – Dessert + tip / About $20 LoL from Rio / Pretzel for appetizer / Apple strudel for dessert]

This 60,000 square-foot replica of Munich's famous Hofbräuhaus offers vats of sauerkraut, beer imported from Bavaria, and best of all a live four-man oompah band, including a tuba, trombone, accordion, and clarinet. They also serve schnitzels, sausages, sauerbraten, and pretzels for a steal. During Bavarian Hour, from 4 to 6 p.m. Sunday through Thursday, visitors can get 20 percent off drinks.

Hootie and the Blowfish's Shady Grove Lounge
Silverton Casino
3333 Blue Diamond Rd.
(702) 263-7777
www.silvertoncasino.com
No Cover

Owned by rockers Hootie and the Blowfish, this Airstream Trailer houses two mini bowling lanes, billiard tables, 12 plasma screens to watch all the sports action, and lots of Hootie memorabilia. Guests can order well drinks and beer for $5 a pop from 4 to 6 p.m.

Jack's Irish Pub
Palace Station
2411 West Sahara Ave.
(702) 367-2411
www.palacestation.com
No Cover

Wooden floors, brick accents, and a wide selection of Irish whiskeys, ales, and ciders make this pub a great place to settle in and enjoy live music, some fish and chips, or karaoke on Wednesday. Booths feature individual televisions making it easy to watch your favorite sporting event anytime. $2 drafts are featured weeknights from 5 to 8 p.m.

Sand Dollar Blues Lounge

3355 Spring Mountain Rd.
(702) 871-6651
www.sanddollarblues.com
No Cover

This blues bar showcases good local live music nightly and is open 24 hours. Enjoy drinks for a song, from $3 to $4, as well as an endless lineup of local and visiting blues and jazz musicians at the city's oldest live music venue.

ALTERNATIVE VENUES FOR MUSIC

College of Southern Nevada

Performing Arts Center
6375 West Charleston Blvd.
(702) 651-5483
www.csn.edu
Free to $12

Catch musical performances by students, professionals, and special guest artists at really reasonable prices (some are even free!). Tickets to see big bands, jazz, and plays at this 525-seat theater only run up to $12 and parking is free.

Fremont Street Concerts

First and Third Street Stages, Pedestrian Promenade
www.vegas4locals.com/freefremontstreetconcerts.html

Head downtown for over a dozen free concerts each month held on the First and Third Street stages along the pedestrian promenade. Most are tribute bands covering Van Halen, Aerosmith, Led Zeppelin, and other rockers, but check the schedule online to find specific info.

Lakeside Music Series

Montelago Village Resort
30 Strada Di Villaggio
(702) 564-4700
www.montelagovillage.com
No Cover

Free weekend concerts featuring tribute bands, classic rock, and jazz groups are performed on the water's edge from 7 to 10 p.m.

University of Nevada Performing Arts Center

Artemus W. Ham Concert Hall
4505 Maryland Pkwy.
(702) 895-2787
www.unlv.edu
From $8 to $30

Enjoy everything from Bach to ballet at this large 1,800-seat theater with excellent acoustics and a lobby full of fine art.

PUBLIC **CONCERTS** AND **FESTIVALS**

Extreme Thing Sports and Music Festival

Desert Breeze Skate Park
8245 Spring Mountain Rd.
www.extremething.com
Tickets from $15

All the action of extreme sports mixed with killer music can be found at this unique event for thrill seekers. Where else but in Vegas could you see BMX dirt jumping, professional wrestling, roller derby and great rock and indie bands all on one day? The festival is in March each year; check the Web site to find out the exact dates.

Las Vegas City of Lights Jazz Rhythm and Blues Festival
Clark County Government Amphitheater
(800) 969-VEGAS
www.yourjazz.com
$60 per adult ticket; children get in free

Celebrating its 18th year, the Las Vegas City of Lights Jazz Rhythm and Blues Festival brings soulful sounds from musicians across the country and the world at this all day and night Saturday event in April. For less than a two-hour show on the Strip, you can groove to live music for 24 hours. Despite the seemingly steep ticket price, children 12 and under get in free, so if you're traveling with the family this festival could be a real bargain.

Viva Las Vegas Rockabilly Weekend
Orleans Hotel
4500 West Tropicana Ave.
www.vivalasvegas.net
Tickets from $89 for all four days

The largest rockabilly weekend in the world, Viva Las Vegas allows lovers of Americana and Elvis to live out their 1950s fantasies. They come to dance the bop, the stroll, and the jive to the endless stream of live bands. There's free dance lessons, a vintage car show, burlesque and fashion shows, a tiki party, and loads of great '50s-rooted sounds and styles. Less than $90 gets you into all the action for four days; at about 23 bucks a day, that's a deal!

COMEDY:
CHEAP JOKES

*"Comedy may be big business
but it isn't pretty."*
—STEVE MARTIN

For those who don't see the humor in losing money at the blackjack table, attending a comedy show or going to a club might be just the thing. If you can't afford the famous shows going for a C-note and up per ticket that have TV programs named after them (Seinfeld, Jay Leno, etc.), there are still some affordable acts to be found on the Strip.

AFFORDABLE **COMEDY** ON **THE** STRIP

Anthony Cools Experience
Paris Hotel
3655 Las Vegas Blvd. South
(877) 374-7469
www.parislasvegas.com
$52, dark on Mon

Raw, racy, uncensored, and extreme. Anthony Cools brings his uninhibited brand of humor to his own six-night-a-week stage show at the Paris resort. Definitely not for kids or the easily offended, his interactive show hypnotizes about a dozen people nightly, delving into audience members' carnal desires. Don't fall asleep, because you may miss something hilarious, or you might wake up to find you were part of the act.

Carrot Top
Luxor
3900 Las Vegas Blvd. South
(702) 262-4400
www.luxor.com
$49, Wed to Mon

Definitely not your garden variety comedian, Carrot Top (aka Scott Thompson) combines trunk loads of crazy props and a spectacle of lights, lasers, and music. Gags come at a machine gun clip and it all ends with a 10-minute encore of rock star impressions of Springsteen, the Rolling Stones, and Kiss.

Dr. Scott Lewis, Outrageous Comedy Hypnotist

Riviera
Le Bistro Theater
2901 Las Vegas Blvd. South
(702) 794-9433
www.rivierahotel.com
$23, Mon nights

Ever want to be a Victoria's Secret model or a pop superstar? Here's your chance to live out the dream . . . except it's in front of a hundred people and you won't remember a thing. Over the course of an hour, chiropractor and fitness counselor Scott Lewis hypnotizes people onstage.

Frank Caliendo

Monte Carlo
Lance Burton Theater
3600 Las Vegas Blvd. South
(720) 730-7000
www.montecarlo.com
$59, Mon, Tues, Fri, and Sat

High energy observational comedy and fast-paced impressions of non-singing celebrities, sports, and political figures—George Bush, Pacino, Dr. Phil, DeNiro, Trump, Leno, John Madden, and Mike Tyson can be found at this 80-minute show, which includes a live four-man band.

Gordie Brown

Golden Nugget
129 Fremont St.
(866) 946-5336
www.goldennugget.com
$39.95, Tues through Sat

Watch as impressionist Gordie Brown transforms into over 40 celebrities including Clint Eastwood, Gary Shandling, Robert DeNiro, and Tom Cruise. Complete with a five-man backup band.

Hypnosis Unleashed

Tropicana
3801 Las Vegas Blvd. South
(702) 739-2222
www.troplv.com
$40, 9 p.m. daily

Bad boys Terry Stokes and Michael Johns entertain crowds as unsuspecting audience members become part of the show and are put in a trance.

Mesmerized

V Theater
Planet Hollywood
3663 Las Vegas Blvd. South
(702) 932-1818
www.varietytheater.com
$49.99, Sat through Thurs

Marc Savard and his assistant Jacky Pagone hypnotize a dozen audience members in between showgirl numbers and comedy routines. See the show or be the show, your choice!

Vinnie Favorito

Flamingo
Bugsy's Cabaret
3555 Las Vegas Blvd. South
(702) 733-3333
www.flamingolasvegas.com
$54, nightly

Audience members are sitting ducks as comedian Vinnie Favorito makes up jokes on the spot during his nightly show at the Flamingo. It doesn't matter where you sit in the 220-seat theater, he will find you. Favorito takes no prisoners with his classic Don Rickles-esque performances, full of wiseguy sass awash in ethnic stereotypes. No two shows are ever the same.

COMEDY **CLUBS** AND **IMPROV** NIGHTS

Bonkerz Comedy Club
Palace Station
2411 Sahara Ave.
(702) 367-2411
www.palacestation.com
$29.95, Thurs 8 p.m., Fri and Sat 8 and 10 p.m.

You'll go bonkers as some of the funniest comics in the country take the stage, including up and coming comedians. Get an hour of two comedians doing funny standup for about 30 bucks instead of wasting it on a few hands of blackjack, all at the location of the notorious OJ Simpson armed-robbery-gone-bad fiasco. Nevada residents get $10 off; just show them your license at the door.

Comedy Stop
Sahara
2535 Las Vegas Blvd. South
(702) 737-2654
www.saharalasvegas.com
$24.95, daily at 7 and 10 p.m.

Since 1983, the Comedy Stop has found and cultivated the best comics in the country including Tim Allen, Rosie O'Donnell, Drew Carey, and Ray Romano. The 650-seat room is open nightly with three new acts each week.

The Improv
Harrah's
3475 Las Vegas Blvd. South
(702) 369-5111
www.harrahslasvegas.com
$24.95; dinner and show $54.95
Tues through Sun, 8:30 and 10:30 p.m.

The Sin City location of this New York City comedy club franchise includes the Big Apple's red-brick background but is not really improv. It's three new up and coming comedians each week performing at the top of their game.

Jest Serendipity Improv Comedy Show

Las Vegas Arts Theater
3330 East Tropicana Rd.
(702) 450-3737
$20, Fri and Sat, 7 p.m.; Sun, 4 and 7 p.m.

Cheer on your favorite team as improv comics battle it out in a head-to-head comedy showdown at Jest Serendipity, the longest running improv comedy show in the desert. No two shows are the same as the unscripted and unrehearsed material is based on audience suggestions.

The LA Comedy Club

Four Queens
202 Fremont St.
(702) 387-5175
www.fourqueens.com
$24.95, Wed, Thurs, and Sun 8:30 p.m.
Fri and Sat, 7:30 and 8:30 p.m.

Nationally known comics perform nightly with new acts rotating in each week. The best, hippest, and brightest entertainers on the circuit provide a great mix of comedy styles without breaking the bank.

The Riviera Comedy Club

Rivera Hotel
Mardi Gras Theater
2901 South Las Vegas Blvd.
(702) 734-5110
www.rivierahotel.com
$32.95, nightly at 8:30 and 10 p.m.

Reminiscent of a Manhattan nightclub, this small comedy venue features headliner comedians as well as ventriloquists and hypnotists. A bit divey and definitely not the Bellagio (this is the Riviera after all), but for comedy on a budget it's good for a night of chuckles.

MAGIC:
CHEAP TRICKS

*"Every morning I get up and look through the
Forbes list of the richest people in America.
If I'm not there, I go to work."*

—MAGICIAN ROBERT ORBEN

Las Vegas is the most magical place this side of Oz, with acts ranging from low-budget kid friendly afternoon shows to high-end 90-minute big stage productions. In the town where every visitor counts on a bit of lady luck to see them through, getting cheap tickets for a magic show might seem like an illusion. Here are some options where no sleight of hand is required.

LOW-COST **SHOWS**

The Mac King Show of Comedy
Harrah's
Comedy Cabaret
3475 Las Vegas Blvd. South
(702) 369-5000
www.harrahslasvegas.com
$24.95, Tues through Sat 1 and 3 p.m.

This unique act contains an unusual combination of quirky humor, visual gags, and amazing sleight of hand. Don't let the beat-up suitcase and gigantic plaid suit influence you; although this show doesn't feature big cats or scantily clad assistants, it still delivers killer deceptions.

Nathan Burton Comedy Magic
Flamingo
3555 Las Vegas Blvd. South
(702) 733-3333
www.flamingolasvegas.com
$34, Tues, Wed, Fri, Sat, Sun

Burton's hour-long act builds humor into classic style illusions with lots of showgirl assistants to lend a helping hand. If you want edgy comedy or tiger action, keep looking, but for one-stop shopping that incorporates all the basics of a solid magic show, this is the ticket.

Rick Thomas

Sahara
2535 Las Vegas Blvd. South
(702) 737-2515
www.saharalasvegas.com
$39.95, 7 p.m. daily

Offering a sparse and swift overview of the latest stage trickery, Thomas's kid-friendly show includes a series of box-bound tricks accented by a bit of dancing from a trio of assistants. Tigers and birds make appearances.

Steven Best and Cassandra—Superstars of Magic

Vegas Club
18 East Fremont St.
(702) 386-2464
$39.95, Wed through Mon, 8:30 p.m.

This high-energy off-the-Strip magic and illusion show features exotic birds, comedy, sleight of hand, and dazzling costumes.

Xtreme Magic Starring Dirk Arthur

Tropicana
3801 Las Vegas Blvd. South
(702) 739-2411
www.troplv.com
$25, Tues through Sat, 4 and 6 p.m.

Dirk Arthur isn't the top cat in magic in Sin City, but now that Siegfried and Roy are out of commission his tigers are now the big dogs on the Strip. His show is one of the only places to see exotic tigers once synonymous with "Vegas style magic." In addition to tricks with the giant hairballs, he includes illusions and sleight of hand in his quick 60-minute show. Well worth the price of admission.

MAGIC **SHOPS**

Denny & Lee Magic Studio
5115 Dean Martin Dr.
(702) 740-3500
www.dennymagic.com

Unlike shops that cater to the practical joke crowd, Denny's sells nothing but magic with a huge inventory of books and videotapes. Employees perform card tricks and other acts of prestidigitation at no charge.

Houdini's Magic Shop
MGM Grand, 3799 Las Vegas Blvd. South
The Forum at Caesars Palace, 3500 Las Vegas Blvd. South
Circus Circus, 2880 Las Vegas Blvd. South
Buffalo Bill's, 31700 Las Vegas Blvd. South
The Venetian, 3355 Las Vegas Blvd. South
www.houdini.com

This chain of magic shops harkens back to master magician Harry Houdini with employees who provide free demonstrations that entertain and entrance visitors. Ten- to fifteen-minute shows materialize every half hour, so if you've got magic on your mind but pennies in your pocket go for the free shows.

Little Shop of Magic
4160 South Durango Dr., #210
(702) 307-6127
www.shopofmagic.com

There's no illusion here; this is a little shop crammed full of tricks, books, and videos, plus a large collection of card and board games.

DANCE:
FOOTLOOSE AND FREE
IN THE DESERT

*"Work like you don't need the money.
Love like you've never been hurt.
Dance like nobody's watching."*

—SATCHEL PAIGE

Big. Bold. Sexy. These singular adjectives befit the chic dance clubs of Las Vegas—hotspots that also tend to go by a singular moniker—Tryst. Bank. Jet. Pure. *Expensive* is another adjective reflective of these exotic nighttime jewels, where dropping a grand or more a night for the privilege of dancing, throwing back a few cocktails, and having a seat for respite is often the norm. If serious dancing and mingling with the beautiful people is what you crave, the clubs below offer free and discounted admission on certain nights of the week so even cheap bastards can get their groove on.

NIGHTCLUBS

Blue Martini
6593 Las Vegas Blvd., Suite 214
(702) 949-2583
www.bluemartinilounge.com
Open 4 p.m. to 3 a.m. nightly
$5 cover

This local watering hole, restaurant, and nightclub is a hip spot to hang off of the Strip. Try one of their 34 varieties of martinis, which are always half off during happy hour, from 4 to 8 p.m. nightly.

Blush
Wynn
3131 South Las Vegas Blvd.
(877) 321-9966
www.wynnlasvegas.com
Open 10 p.m. to 4 a.m., Tues and Thurs to Sat
Local ladies always free, free for locals Tues nights

This 4,500-square-foot boutique nightclub is smaller than most on the Strip and includes an outside garden area, onyx dance floor lit by multicolored lights, and contemporary paintings providing an upscale vibe. Definitely a worthy alternative to the usual Las Vegas clubs as here you can park yourself for a rest at one of the many seating areas without being required to hand over your mortgage payment for a minimum bottle purchase.

Coyote Ugly

New York New York
3790 Las Vegas Blvd. South
(702) 740-6969
www.nynyhotelcasino.com
Open 6 p.m. to 2 a.m. nightly
Free from 6 to 9 p.m., locals free all night every night

You've seen the bad movie, now experience the 2,500-square-foot saloon, one of the loudest and rowdiest in town. A favorite of the younger set, the bar features the celebrated scantily clad coyotes, seriously limber ambidextrous flair bartenders who can mix, pour, and serve drinks from every imaginable position while dancing atop the longest bar west of the Mississippi. Join in and dance or leave something behind for the famous Bra Wall of Fame.

House of Blues

Mandalay Bay
3950 Las Vegas Blvd. South
(702) 632-7777
www.mandalaybay.com
Open 11 p.m. to 4 a.m. nightly
Local ladies always free

The 1,800-seat Las Vegas House of Blues carries the brand's legacy of providing an eclectic mix of live music acts in a unique setting, integrating music, dancing, dining, and retail. The three-story, 40,000-square-foot venue also hosts their mainstay Sunday gospel brunch, where a double helping of cheddar cheese grits is served up with live hand-clapping gospel music.

Moon

Palms Hotel
4321 West Flamingo Rd.
(702) 942-7777
www.palms.com
Open 10 p.m. to 4 a.m., Tues and Thurs to Sun

This 12,500-square-foot club is all about a hip-hop groove and some very serious dancing. The club boasts a white, steel, silver, and glass moon-surface decor with a retractable roof. Metallic space-suited go-go boot wearing staff serve up overpriced libations. Get an All Access Pass to gain entry to Moon, Ghostbar, and the Playboy Club for just $25 Tues and Thurs.

Risque

Paris
3645 Las Vegas Blvd. South
(877) 603-4386
www.parislasvegas.com
Open 10:30 p.m. to 4 a.m., Fri and Sat
Local ladies always free

This post-modern Eurasian multi-level club offers secluded seating areas and tables around the dance floor if you want to be near the center of the action. Make your way to one of the six balconies for a nice view of the Strip and Bellagio fountains. Guests of the hotel get free entry passes, so make sure to ask for them at check-in.

TAO

Venetian
3355 South Las Vegas Blvd.
(702) 444-1000
www.venetian.com
Open 10:30 p.m. to 4 a.m., Thurs through Sat
Locals free on Thurs nights

The Far East meets New York chic in this 10,000-square-foot beauty of a club. A 20-foot-tall Buddha welcomes guests to the massive club decorated with rock gardens, soothing candles, and stone statuary. The main dance floor is situated on a raised platform, so be aware that everyone can see your worst dance moves.

Voodoo Lounge

Rio
3700 West Flamingo Rd.
(866) 746-7671
www.riolasvegas.com
Open 5 p.m. to 3 a.m. nightly
Local ladies always free

Perched on the 51st floor, you can enjoy an intimate evening of dancing and drinking at this elegantly appointed club. Flair bartenders provide plenty of eye candy and you can get a spectacular glimpse of the city from the cozy indoors as well as the comfy outdoor terrace area.

PLACES **TO** SWING **AND** DANCE

Aruba Swings
Aruba Hotel
1215 Las Vegas Blvd. South
(702) 383-3100
www.arubalasvegas.com
Second and fourth Friday each month
Free

Cut a rug at the legendary Thunderbird Lounge on alternating Friday nights at the Aruba Hotel. A free beginners swing dancing lesson is offered before the jiving begins.

Las Palmas Restaurant
953 East Sahara Ave., Suite A-27
(702) 732-0010

Wednesday nights swing inside this Mexican restaurant. There's a free lesson before open dance begins so if you get there early you can enjoy some great cheap grub and then work off all those extra calories.

Tuscany
255 East Flamingo Rd.
(702) 893-8933
www.tuscanylasvegas.com
Open Wed and Sat starting at 8 p.m.

Head to the small bar at the Tuscany Hotel to to strut your stuff in style every Wednesday and Saturday night. It's also ladies night every Wednesday, so drinks are half price for all the gals.

DANCE **PERFORMANCES**

Nevada Ballet Theatre
1651 Inner Circle
(702) 243-2623
www.nevadaballet.com

This training academy and professional ballet company performs a variety of shows ranging from classic works to contemporary ballets. Dancers are recruited from around the globe and the seasonal performances include the classic *Nutcracker* and a unique Choreographer's Showcase with original pieces including Cirque du Soleil dancers. The theater offers an introductory series subscription to select performances for only $20.

University of Las Vegas
Judy Bayley Theatre
Dance One Studio
4505 South Maryland Pkwy.
(702) 895-2787
www.unlv.edu

The University of Las Vegas's dance program features a mix of performances by faculty, staff, and guest artists. Classical ballet and experimental modern works are represented. Check their schedule for shows; tickets are $18 for the general public and $10 for students and seniors.

GAMBLING:
CHEAP BETS

"Someone once asked me why women don't gamble as much as men do, and I gave the common-sensical reply that we don't have as much money. That was a true but incomplete answer. In fact, women's total instinct for gambling is satisfied by marriage."

—GLORIA STEINEM

Feeling lucky? Gambling is the only game in town. A visit to Sin City just wouldn't be complete without taking in the casino scene.

But beware, once you enter a casino, you might never find your way out. It's a labyrinthine maze of slot machines, craps tables, and blackjack dealers. There are no clocks (so you lose track of time) and no windows (so you can't tell you've actually been on the casino floor for three whole days). If you stick to a few rules you should be able to do some gambling and keep your shirt:

- Wait until you've at least arrived at your hotel before spending—then you can do it in a comfy chair with a free drink in your hand.

- Unlike in the film *Indecent Proposal,* there are a few if any Robert Redford look-alikes milling about to bail you out of your financial woes. Take a watch and set a time to leave.

- Never bet more than you can lose, so budget how much you are willing to spend for the fun of it and when it's gone leave the casino floor.

- Before you hit the tables, learn the games. Major casinos issue free how-to booklets and lessons to attract potential players.

Most of us would like to leave Las Vegas rich, but usually that doesn't happen no matter how much we gamble. So, why not gamble cheap?

PLAYER **CLUBS**

Who hasn't dreamed of rolling into town with nothing, like Tom Cruise in *Rain Man,* and getting comped a penthouse suite at Caesars overlooking the twinkling lights of the Strip? Well, dream on. It doesn't often happen to penny pinchers.

Comps (short for complimentary) are the freebies—rooms, meals, and show tickets—that casinos hand out to serious players. Usually these are given to the big spenders, but there is a way for a cheap bastard to get in on some of the action without breaking the bank.

Every major casino and most of the smaller ones have some form of a player tracking system, aka a players club. This enables the casino to know who their players are, track what games they play, and reward them appropriately—with the goal of gaining additional action.

Players who sign up for a club membership **(always for free)** are given a plastic card that they insert into card readers on each machine. As you play you can earn points. The secret here is that many casinos give you automatic benefits just for signing up for the card. These can include a dollar amount of free slot play, room upgrades, and discounts on restaurants and shows. Basically only a dummy would pass that up. The machines are going to pay you the same whether you use a card or not—so why not get some additional rewards along the way?

✓ **Binion's** —
128 Fremont St.
(702) 382-1600
www.binions.com

Join Club Binion's for free or receive $25 in slot play or table game chips and a photo with the $1 million display for just $2. Members also receive preferential consideration when booking rooms, food and beverage discounts, and invitations to VIP events. Every 40 points earned equals $1 cash back and $2 in comp dollars.

Boyd Gaming and Coast Casinos
California
12 East Ogden
(702) 385-1222
www.thecal.com

✓ **Fremont** —
200 Fremont St.
(702) 385-3232
www.fremontcasino.com

Gold Coast
4000 West Flamingo Rd.
(702) 367-7111
www.goldcoastcasino.com

Main Street Station
200 North Main St.
(702) 387-1896
www.mainstreetcasino.com

The Orleans
4500 West Tropicana
(702) 365-7111
www.orleanscasino.com

Sam's Town
5111 Boulder Hwy.
(702) 456-7777
www.samstownlv.com

Suncoast
9090 Alta Dr.
(702) 636-7111
www.coastcasinos.com

One card does it all at Suncoast, The Orleans, Gold Coast, and Sam's Town as well as California, Fremont, and Main Street Station downtown. Each tier—ruby, sapphire, and emerald—offers an increasingly valuable series of services and benefits including qualifying for dining, room, and gift shop discounts as well as special event invitations.

Casino Royale
3411 Las Vegas Blvd. South
(702) 737-3500
www.casinoroyalehotel.com

Joining the Club Royale is the player's path to free meals, slot play discounts, and complimentary room rates. Club members receive free rooms, triple points offered twice daily, and $50 in slot play and bonus coupons for cash bonuses and free drinks for new members.

Club Riviera
2901 Las Vegas Blvd. South
(702) 794-9441
www.rivierahotel.com

The convenient location offers three-tiered rewards for play and loyalty, leading up to discounts at restaurants, retail shops, spas, and shows. Additionally, members receive up to $1,000 in free slot play, free transportation to and from the airport, and comp rooms.

see pg 66-67

El Cortez

Old Vegas Downtown

600 Fremont St.
(702) 385-5200
www.ecvegas.com

Any Club Cortez member earning 500 Club Points in a single day is eligible to play in the $500 daily slot tournament the following day. Members receive double points Tuesday and Thursday and up to half-off discounts at the hotel's Flame Steakhouse.

Encore and Wynn

3131 Las Vegas Blvd. South
(702) 770-7171
(877) 321-9966
www.wynnlasvegas.com

The Red Card is not only the key to your room but also your way to access extra-special service. Secure reservations to restaurants, shows, and tee times. Red Card members also receive regular promotional room rates including discounts up to 50 percent.

Fitzgeralds

Old Vegas Downtown

301 Fremont St.
(702) 388-2400
www.fitzgeraldslasvegas.com

Join Club Fitz and earn one point for every $5 in play on slots and video keno and one point of every $10 of video poker play. Members earn 1 point for every $5 and for every 100 points members receive $1 cash back.

Golden Nugget

Old Vegas Downtown

129 Fremont St.
(702) 385-7111
www.goldennugget.com

Join the 24 Karat Club and spin to win up to $1,000 in free slot play. Other rewards include meals, rooms, and shows; special room rates; VIP reservation service; and invitations to parties and events.

Hard Rock Hotel

4455 Paradise Rd.
(800) 473-7625
www.hardrockhotel.com

Anybody can be a rock star by joining the Hard Rock's players club—the best way to get tickets to concerts, access to clubs, and free slot and table play. Members can receive Hard Rock merchandise and premium items from their Rockstar gift catalogue as well as direct mail offers on reduced room rates. Each 500 points translates to $1 cash back.

Harrah's Entertainment

Bally's
✓
3645 Las Vegas Blvd. South
(877) 603-4390
www.ballyslasvegas.com

Caesars Palace
✓
3570 Las Vegas Blvd. South
(866) 227-5938
www.caesarspalace.com

Flamingo
3555 Las Vegas Blvd. South
(702) 733-3111
www.flamingolasvegas.com

Harrah's
✓
3475 Las Vegas Blvd. South
www.harrahslasvegas.com
(800) 214-9110

Imperial Palace
3535 Las Vegas Blvd. South
(702) 731-3311
www.imperialpalace.com

Paris
✓
3655 Las Vegas Blvd. South
(877) 603-4386
www.parislasvegas.com

Rio
3700 West Flamingo Rd.
(866) 746-7671
www.riolasvegas.com

In a few minutes you can sign up for the Total Rewards card at a casino promotions booth at Harrah's, Caesars Palace, Imperial Palace, Rio, Paris, Bally's, or the Flamingo. Play in any of these casinos will earn credits towards becoming a gold, platinum, diamond, or seven bar member. Each tier provides discounts on a variety of venues, including the Forum Shops, wedding chapels, spas, and show tickets as well as free birthday gifts and offers and discounted and complimentary golf.

Hooters
115 East Tropicana
(702) 739-9000
www.hooterscasinohotel.com

Earn Owl Rewards points playing your favorite casino or slot games then turn the points into cash and Hooters swag. Sign up and get a Hooters coupon book including $100 in free slot play. Points earned can be used for Hooters T-shirts, mugs, and sweatshirts as well as iPods, TVs, and cruises.

M Resort
12300 Las Vegas Blvd. South
(702) 797-1000
www.themresort.com

Join the iMagine Players Club and get a free T-shirt, $5 in play, and other rewards. Members receive one point on every $1 of play as well as restaurant and room discounts, and VIP free passes to shows and concerts.

Planet Hollywood
3667 Las Vegas Blvd. South
(702) 785-5555
www.planethollywood.com

Join the A-list Players Club and receive your free Guide to the Planet Reward Book, featuring gifts, dining, and shopping discounts worth more than $3,000. As part of the Harrah's chain, in addition to the rewards book, members receive all the benefits provided to Harrah's Player Card holders.

Free Gaming Lessons

Many of the bigger casinos offer free lessons for table games. This is an excellent way to get over your initial fear of sitting down to a new game. Usually the lesson entails an explanation of how the game is played and the rules and procedures that you need to know. Some lessons also include a "fake" free game using "funny money" or non-value chips. By playing these practice hands you can get a real feel for the flow of the game before losing your shirt.

Bally's
3645 Las Vegas Blvd. South
(877) 603-4390
www.ballyslasvegas.com
Poker, 9:30 a.m
Mon through Fri

Binion's
128 Fremont St.
(702) 382-1600
www.binions.com
Poker, 11 a.m.
Daily

Circus Circus
2880 Las Vegas Blvd. South
(702) 734-0410
www.circuscircus.com
Blackjack, 10:30 a.m.
Roulette, 11 a.m.
Craps, 11:30 a.m.
Mon through Fri

Fitzgeralds
301 Fremont St.
(702) 388-2400
www.fitzgeraldslasvegas.com
Poker, 10 a.m.
Daily

Golden Nugget
129 Fremont St.
(702) 385-7111
www.goldennugget.com
✓ Craps, 10 a.m. and noon
Poker, 10 a.m.
Roulette, 11:30 a.m.
Blackjack, noon
Daily

Imperial Palace
3535 Las Vegas Blvd. South
(702) 731-3311
www.imperialpalace.com
Poker, 7 a.m. and 11 a.m.
Blackjack, 9 a.m.
Roulette, 10 a.m.
Craps, 10 a.m.
Mon through Fri

Las Vegas Hilton
3000 Paradise Rd.
(702) 732-5111
www.lvhilton.com
Craps, 10:30 a.m. and 4 p.m.
Blackjack, 2 p.m.
Poker, 3 and 5 p.m.
Mon through Fri

Luxor
3900 Las Vegas Blvd. South
(702) 262-4400
www.luxor.com
Poker, 9 a.m. and 2 p.m.
Daily

Mandalay Bay
3950 Las Vegas Blvd. South
(702) 632-9500
www.mandalaybay.com
Poker, 2 p.m.
Mon through Thurs

Palms
4321 West Flamingo Rd.
(702) 942-7777
www.palms.com
Poker, noon
Mon through Fri

Planet Hollywood Resort
3667 Las Vegas Blvd. South
(702) 785-5555
www.planethollywood.com
Poker, 9 a.m.
Blackjack, 10 a.m.
Craps, 11 a.m.
Roulette, 12:30 p.m.
Baccarat, 1:15 p.m.
Mon through Fri

Stratosphere
2000 Las Vegas Blvd. South
(702) 380-7707
www.stratospherehotel.com
Poker, 8:30 a.m.
Daily

Tropicana
3801 Las Vegas Blvd. South
(702) 739-2222
www.troplv.com
Poker, 10 a.m.
Daily

The Venetian
3355 Las Vegas Blvd. South
(702) 414-1000
www.venetian.com
Craps, 11 a.m. and 5 p.m.
Roulette, noon
Blackjack, 12:15 p.m.
Mon through Fri

Plaza and Vegas Club

1 South Main St.
(702) 386-2110
www.vegasclubcasino.com

The member program boasts more choices and more rewards, especially within 24 hours of sign-up; free slot play, T-shirts, and buffets. Members earning 500 points get $1 cash back or $1.50 in free slot play. New members can receive up to $250 in comps their first day of play.

Sahara

2535 Las Vegas Blvd. South
(702) 737-2654
www.saharalasvegas.com

Every 100 points earned means $5 cash back and $5 EZ Money, plus comp dollars at Paco's Bar and Grill and other restaurants. Members can also participate in the daily free pull for a chance at $10,000.

Silverton

3333 Blue Diamond Rd.
(702) 263-7777
www.silvertoncasino.com

The Discover Club offers comp dollars for meals, hotel accommodations, and concert tickets. Every 500 points earn 1 comp dollar good throughout the casino.

South Point

9777 Las Vegas Blvd. South
(702) 796-7111
www.southpointcasino.com

Every dollar you play equals one point at the Club and 4,000 points equals $12 in cash back comps and free play.

Station Casinos

www.stationcasinos.com

Boarding Pass Guest Rewards Program members are eligible for discounts on dining, entertainment, and rooms as well as Jumbo-branded progressive jackpots. Members who acquire 1,000 points earn $1 in cash back or comps.

The Venetian and The Palazzo

3355 Las Vegas Blvd. South
(702) 414-1000
www.palazzolasvegas.com

Gifts from Club Grazie include shopping sprees and VIP discounts to entertainment, accommodation, dining, gondola rides, retail outlets, and nightlife. Each slot reward point earns one Grazie gift point and new members receive $15 in free slot play.

CHEAP **TABLES** AND **SLOTS**

A good rule to remember is the classier the casino, the more of the big money slots and tables it has. If you want to stretch your bankroll, you'll have to go out to Boulder Highway where they cater to locals, or head downtown to the older casinos where they do whatever they can to bring in business. You'll find some dollar blackjack and quarter craps and roulette at many of the Fremont Street casinos and that might be incentive enough to venture within.

Casino Royale

3411 Las Vegas Blvd. South
(702) 737-3500
www.casinoroyalehotel.com

Don't let its location next to the Venetian fool you—Casino Royale is small, dingy, and cheap. It offers $2 blackjack and $3 craps.

Eldorado

2950 Industrial Rd.
(702) 564-1811
www.eldoradocasino.com

Located in Old Town Henderson, this really cheap casino offers up some $2 blackjack tables as well as inexpensive roulette.

Joker's Wild

920 North Boulder Hwy.
(702) 564-8100
www.jokerswildcasino.com

Also in Henderson, the Joker's Wild lies on a deserted stretch on Boulder Highway, enticing locals with cheap $2 blackjack tables. They also offer $1 craps tables until midnight with 10x odds and roulette as low as a quarter.

Klondike Sunset

444 West Sunset Rd.
(702) 568-7575

The third bargain blackjack place in Henderson, this casino isn't glamorous or pretty to look at but if you are pinching pennies you can find some 2-buck tables.

The Longhorn

5288 North Boulder Hwy.
(702) 435-9170

This smoky small casino also offers cheap blackjack, so if you aren't claustrophobic or asthmatic you can get your gamble on for $2.

The Plaza

1 South Main St.
(702) 386-2110
www.plazahotelcasino.com

This downtown spot has a funky vibe and if you go looking long enough you'll find $3 craps and blackjack tables.

Poker Palace

2757 Las Vegas Blvd. North
(702) 649-3799
wwww.pokerpalace.net

Located in unsavory North Las Vegas, this small and dingy casino offers some $1 blackjack tables.

Sahara *closed 5/16/11*

2535 Las Vegas Blvd. South
(702) 737-2654
www.saharalasvegas.com

In addition to their more than 2,500 slot and video poker games, the Sahara still offers some $1 blackjack tables.

Slots-O-Fun

2890 Las Vegas Blvd. South
(702) 734-0410

This dingy outpost next door to Circus Circus has some cheap $2 games but you usually have to wait a while to get in on the action. They also have dollar craps and quarter and 50 cent roulette. At least this location is on the Strip and you can get a decent free cocktail while you play.

SECTION 2:

Exploring & Living in Las Vegas

CHEAP SLEEPS
FOR TRAVELERS

*"People who sleep like a baby
usually don't have one."*

—LEO J. BURKE

Vegas was a toddler during the Great Depression and was generally immune to its snake-eyed wrath. Not so with the current financial crunch. Today, the new reality is that you can have a nice long weekend lolling around at a pool in a desert hotel at unemployment compensation rates. Cheap is a relative term in Sin City, as what is $300 per night on a weekend or during a busy convention can be $99 on a boring Wednesday night.

If you follow a few basic rules, you can find reasonably priced accommodations for good rates—we aren't talking Bellagio and Encore here, but a hotel with a toilet and bed, and clean enough that you aren't waking up with the roaches.

If you are not driving into town, often your best bet is a package deal, although the most attractive prices mean that you may be taking a crowded flight at an inconvenient time and your hotel room may be way, way off the Strip.

The best time to look for hotel room bargains is about a month before your trip. The hotels have a good idea how many vacancies they have and they will be adjusting prices to get empty rooms filled. Remember that free players club we urged you to sign up for in the gambling chapter? Well, that comes in handy here. Call the number on the card instead of the general 1-800 reservation number and see if you can get a special rate.

Before you go, set aside an hour and call 15 or 20 casinos. It doesn't cost anything to comparison shop because casino 1-800 reservation numbers are all toll free. Also check the hotel Web sites as they often offer better rates than their reservation lines. This way you can get a good idea for prices at the hotels in which you know you are interested.

Remember, the farther from the Strip you are, the cheaper the rooms will be. You can usually find a room for $30 to $60 at one of the downtown or Boulder Highway hotels.

It's best to leave on a Monday, Tuesday, or Wednesday as you can take advantage of lower midweek hotel rates. Rates for weekdays are generally about half the price of weekends. The cheapest times to travel during the year are the weeks before Christmas in December and in the middle of the summer during July or August. Stay clear of holiday weekends and major conventions, when hotel room rates soar.

Rates here were current at press time, but be sure to call ahead before traveling to confirm.

GETTING **TO** THE **STRIP**

✓ **McCarran International Airport**
757 Wayne Newton Blvd.
(702) 261-5211
www.mccarran.com

If you're staying on the Strip or downtown, getting to your hotel is a cinch. Taxis, shuttles, limos, and buses are all available from the airport. Shuttles are inexpensive and Bell Trans (800-274-7433) runs 20 passenger SUVs daily from 7:45 a.m. to midnight between the airport and all major hotels and resorts. Shuttles depart outside the airport, west of the baggage claim area and costs are approximately $5.50 per person. Even less expensive are CAT local buses, which depart from the airport and drop off riders at the Stratosphere on the Strip, where you can catch the #301 bus, which makes stops close to most hotels. Fares average $2 per adult. You can also opt for a taxi, which runs about $15, or if you want to splurge and spend $40 to $50 you can hire one of the many limos available outside the airport.

OFF-**THE**-STRIP **HOTELS** & **MOTELS**

Aliante Station
7300 Aliante Pkwy.
(800) 851-1703
www.aliantecasinohotel.com
$74 per night, check online specials for cheaper rates

Two hundred rooms decorated in contemporary style, a big casino, race and sports book, six restaurants, and a 16-screen movie theater make Aliante a good bargain at $125 for two nights (online special) with an additional $100 in credits if you book online. Although a 20-minute drive from Strip action, the rooms are very upscale for the price.

Arizona Charlie's Boulder
4575 Boulder Hwy.
(800) 362-4040
www.arizonacharliesboulder.com
$26.99

Arizona Charlie's Decatur
740 South Decatur Blvd.
(800) 342-2695
www.arizonacharliesdecatur.com
$44.99

Most of the 303 (Boulder) and 258 (Decatur) rooms offer a separate living room as well as a bedroom (which is small) and a tiny bathroom. It's bit above your standard Motel 6 room, but the casino is unattached at the Boulder location so be prepared to walk to get your game on. The Decatur location is a bit nicer, although rooms are dimly lit and smoky.

Boulder Station
4111 Boulder Hwy.
(800) 851-1703
www.boulderstation.com
$20.99

Located a few minutes from the Strip and Glitter Gulch, this 300-room hotel offers a huge casino (75,000 square feet) and movie theater, attracting tons of local and blue collar visitors. Rooms are very standard but neat and clean, and for about only 20 bucks what else do you expect?

Ellis Island Super 8
4178 Koval Lane
(702) 733-8901
www.ellisislandcasino.com
$41

Located a block away from the Strip, the Ellis Island's 300 rooms are nicer than a Motel 6 and larger, featuring queen beds. Older clientele flock here for the mega cheap coffee shop food.

Fiesta Henderson
777 West Lake Mead Dr.
(888) 899-7770
www.fiestahendersonlasvegas.com
$26

This small hotel (224 rooms) hints at a Mexican theme but rooms include neutral light wood furniture and carpeting. Local seniors come for the cheap buffet, slots, and air-conditioned movie theater.

The Lowdown on Traveling and Transportation
When to Fly to Las Vegas
There's hardly a bad time to visit Sin City. If you want to avoid the crowds and get a better deal on one of the 25,000 hotel rooms on the Strip, book your trip during the week. If you want the cheapest rates, go in the middle of summer when temperatures and flight and hotel prices sizzle.

Peak Season
Spring and fall are the most pleasant seasons to visit but attract crowds drawn to the city's sunny climate. Visitor population peaks on New Year's Eve, Super Bowl Sunday, Valentine's Day, and pro sporting events such as boxing matches and NCAA basketball championships. These are also the most expensive times to go, so if you can, opt to visit during the off season and save some Benjamins.

Off Season
Climate dictates the decrease in visitors and hotel rates, with July and August temperatures averaging over 100 degrees and offering the best travel deals. Vegas is less crowded between Christmas and New Year's Eve and in the months of January and February, and you can score good deals on flights and rooms. Just as an FYI, although most cities keep their pools open year-round, due to desert winds most outdoor pools are closed from Labor Day to Memorial Day.

Fiesta Rancho
2400 North Rancho Dr.
(800) 731-7333
www.fiestarancholasvegas.com
$19.59

The huge casino is the draw here (100,000 square feet). The hotel only houses 100 rooms and is located in the middle of nowhere. We didn't see anyone under 45 inside, so young'uns should head elsewhere. The skating rink provides a nice break from the smoky casino. Book online and receive up to 40 percent off.

Getting Around

One of the best and cheapest ways to see the Strip is by foot, as heavy traffic lines the street during weekends and rush hour (5 to 8 p.m.). The 301 bus travels between downtown (at Casino Center Boulevard and Stewart Street) and a few miles beyond the southern end of the Strip. The Deuce, a double decker 24-hour bus, runs the length of the Strip, with a $5 all day pass allowing passengers to get on and off as many times as they like. The Las Vegas monorail 4-mile route runs from the MGM Grand to the Sahara, with stops along the way for $5 one way. Operating hours are Monday through Thursday from 7 a.m. to 2 a.m. and Friday to Sunday from 7 a.m. to 3 a.m.

Free Shuttles

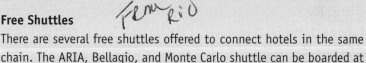

There are several free shuttles offered to connect hotels in the same chain. The ARIA, Bellagio, and Monte Carlo shuttle can be boarded at each of the resorts for rides to the other two MGM properties.

A free monorail also connects Mandalay Bay with Luxor and Excalibur with stops at each hotel.

Parking

Unlike other cities, most Las Vegas hotels offer free valet parking for just the price of a tip ($1 or $2 is fine). Most hotels also have parking garages in the back that are absolutely free, but if you want to save yourself the equivalent of walking several blocks opt for the valet.

Gold Coast
4000 West Flamingo Rd.
(800) 331-5334
www.goldcoastcasino.com
$29

The clean 750 rooms here have modern amenities like flat-screen TVs, irons, and hair dryers for a decent price, $29 per night. Shuttle service makes it easy to get to the Strip and the bowling alley and very cheap restaurants are also a plus. If you book early—61 days out—and online, you can save 15 percent.

Orleans

4500 West Tropicana Ave.
(800) ORLEANS
www.orleanscasino.com
$35

This large (142,000-square-foot) casino and hotel (1,880 rooms) is out in the boonies but has so much stuff to keep you busy you really don't need to go anywhere else. If you don't want to gamble, you can watch the latest flick at the 18-screen movie complex, bowl a few games at their late night bowling alley, visit the spa, or eat at the large food court. The decor in the L-shaped rooms is fake New Orleans with brass headboards and Victorian-like lace curtains.

Palace Station

2411 West Sahara Ave.
(800) 634-3101
www.palacestation.com
$18.95 and up

The Catch Be aware of the mandatory amenity fee that gets tacked on automatically to your room rate.

True penny pinchers can opt for the older "garden" rooms ($18.95) which haven't been updated in a long, long time. The tower rooms ($26.24), which go for a little more, are updated with large flat-screen TVs and modern furnishings and worth the splurge. This hotel is really out in the boonies so you'll have to cab it anywhere else if you are carless.

Terrible's

4100 Paradise Rd.
(800) 640-9777
www.terriblescasinos.com
$34 and up

Located 1 mile off the Strip and close to the airport and a bunch of fairly good restaurants, Terrible's 330 rooms are priced from $34 (standard) up to $134 (suite). Regular standard rooms are large and definitely not terrible for the price. The pool is better than those at most budget hotels. The hotel also offers a free shuttle bus to and from the airport.

Wild Wild West
3300 West Tropicana Ave.
(702) 740-0000
www.wildwildwesthotelcasino.com
$35

Within walking distance to the Strip, this small 260-room hotel is a much cheaper alternative to the pricier resorts a few blocks down. The only fountain you'll see here though is the soda kind at the connecting Denny's. There are lots of truckers, probably because the huge parking lot can fit all their rigs and because it is located right next to a truck stop, so if you want a peaceful slumber pack your earplugs.

DOWNTOWN **HOTELS** & **MOTELS**

California
12 Ogden St.
(800) 634-6255
www.thecal.com
$36

Order anything in "the Cal's" coffee shop and you'll get a side of spam in this island-themed 780-room hotel. Just one block away from Fremont Street, rooms are spacious and moderately priced. Although named after the 31st state, the decor, food, and most of the gamblers are devoted to the 50th state.

El Cortez
600 Fremont St.
(800) 634-6703
www.ecvegas.com
$27

This 308-room hotel is so old school you expect to find Frank and Dean lounging with a drink at the front desk. Rooms come in "vintage" (translation: cheap at $27) and the South Beach flavored "Cabana Suites" across the street. The suites are nicer and pricier ($42), but beware of the lime green color scheme.

Fitzgeralds

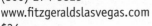

301 Fremont St.
(800) 274-5825
www.fitzgeraldslasvegas.com
$34

Fitzgeralds is a tired old hotel but the 650 rooms are spacious and cheap. As this is one of the tallest buildings downtown try to talk yourself into a higher floor room to enjoy the view. Head to the poker room to watch the Fremont Street Experience while you play hold 'em.

Four Queens

202 East Fremont St.
(800) 634-6045
www.fourqueens.com
$30

You can feel like a queen for a mere 30 quid at this 690-room block-long hotel and casino. Bathrooms are on the very small side and the decor is brash. Noise from Fremont Street is loud and continues until late so bring your earplugs, but for $30 a night what do you expect?

Fremont

200 East Fremont St.
(800) 634-6182
www.fremontcasino.com
$36

The downtown hotel has really small rooms and even smaller bathrooms but they are clean. Lots of Hawaiians gamble here, maybe coming for the variety of Hawaiian-themed restaurants. Paper thin walls and the loud Fremont Experience show below will keep you awake past midnight, but who goes to Vegas to sleep?

Gold Spike

400 East Ogden Ave.
(702) 384-8444
www.goldspike.com
$30

Once known for having a permanent stench of whiskey and a fog of cigarette smoke throughout the property, the Gold Spike recently was renovated and now everything old is new again. New slot machines and all-female dealers. New restaurant where almost everything is under a 10 spot. The new turquoise and brown room decor is a bit bright, but a welcome improvement over the old pre-renovation tired and dingy digs.

Golden Gate

[handwritten: Old Vegas Downtown]   *[handwritten: Also Golden Nugget + Binions]*

1 Fremont St.
(702) 382-3510
www.goldengatecasino.com
$29

Golden Gate offers 106 rooms all done in a newly renovated modern style. Old San Francisco artifacts and decor are woven throughout the hotel, but that's about all the resemblance. The cramped dimly lit hallways and low ceilings can give anyone a bout of claustrophobia. For a truly tacky experience, head to the casino on a weekend night to view the go-go dancers on the tables. Don't forget to try the shrimp cocktail—it was here where the 99-cent tradition began.

Main Street Station

200 Main St.
(800) 465-0711
www.mainstreetcasino.com
$36

This 400-room hotel and casino serves a great microbrew and is two blocks away from Fremont Street. Decor is early 20th-century San Francisco with antique-style chandeliers, dark woods, and stained glass windows. The ornate decorating doesn't extend to the rooms, but they are large, long, and narrow with wood accents.

Vegas Club

18 East Fremont St.
(800) 634-6532
www.vegasclubcasino.com
$29

Really tired rooms with few amenities but the bathrooms are bigger than most offered downtown. Here you really do just get what you pay for at $29 per night. Those carpets aren't dark brown, they are just dirty.

ON-**THE-**STRIP **HOTELS** & **MOTELS**

Casino Royale
3411 Las Vegas Blvd. South
(800) 854-7666
www.casinoroyalehotel.com
$59

Hidden between the Venetian and Harrah's, this hotel houses a dark and smoky casino with loose slots. Great for its location and price, but a bit run-down.

Circus Circus
2880 Las Vegas Blvd. South
(702) 734-0410
www.circuscircus.com
$22

This is the one place in Vegas where there is always an abundance of children running around unsupervised. The "manor" rooms out back are the cheapest but aren't very nice. The tower rooms ($46.95) are a much better choice for a few bucks more with flat-screen TV's, newer furnishings, and bright blue and orange decor. The casino houses an arcade, carnival games, and ongoing free circus acts.

Excalibur
3850 Las Vegas Blvd. South
(877) 750-5464
www.excalibur.com
$36

This large white castle-themed hotel (complete with a moat, drawbridge, and towers) houses over 4,000 rooms. Decorated in an Olde English theme, newer rooms ($56) feature suede headboards, flat-screen TVs, and even marble in the bathroom. The old standard rooms ($36) are just that, really standard with no bells and whistles. Their Web site offers a wide range of promotions, so check before you book.

Sahara

closed 5/16/11

2535 South Las Vegas Blvd.
(702) 737-2654
www.saharalasvegas.com
$25

Featured in the film *Ocean's Eleven* and once the gathering spot for Rat Packers Frank Sinatra and Dean Martin, the Sahara epitomizes old-school Las Vegas. The pool and hotel are huge with each of the 1,700 rooms decorated in a Moroccan theme. Sure, it's old and a tad seedy, but for $25 on the Strip it's still a great bargain. Offering $1 beer, blackjack, and hot dogs, it's cheaper than staying at home. Ask for the coupon book when you check in for discounts on food, rides, and shows.

Stratosphere

2000 Las Vegas Blvd. South
(702) 380-7707
www.stratospherehotel.com
$27.50

You'll have to get your thrills on the X-Scream, Big Shot, and Insanity rides because the plain rooms are nothing to scream about. It's a fairly good location though, with affordable IHOP across the street and two nice pools.

Tropicana

3801 Las Vegas Blvd. South
(702) 739-2222
www.troplv.com
$69

The Catch We hear the Trop is undergoing an expensive renovation to a Miami theme to debut in 2010, so rooms might be nicer but prices might go up.

You'll probably crave a drink with an umbrella after checking into this Caribbean themed hotel. Rooms are clean and fall into three different price ranges; garden rooms are the least expensive at $69 and island and paradise tower rooms are bigger and run upwards of $79. Pluses are location and pool areas.

FOOD:
ON THE HOUSE

"Soup is just a way of screwing you out of a meal."

—JAY LENO

A decade or so ago, Vegas was known for the 99-cent cocktail and the $1.99 steak and eggs. For decades, it was gospel that money could buy you anything in Las Vegas but a good meal. But in the roaring '80s, Sin City went upscale, with restaurants run by famous chefs. The city transformed itself from a food dead zone to what is today touted as "America's next great culinary city." Led by chef-to-the-stars Wolfgang Puck, who brought a version of his see-and-be-seen Hollywood restaurant Spago to Las Vegas in 1992, an army of celebrity chefs has opened outposts. Today, Las Vegas is now as much a destination for serious foodies as for gamblers.

But don't despair—recent worldwide economic turmoil has left Las Vegas down on its luck and that's good news to all hungry and budget-conscious consumers. Savvy, determined travelers can find a wickedly cheap meal on or off the Strip.

CHEAP **BUFFETS**

Las Vegas is the buffet capital of the world, with more than 100 casino buffets ranging from cheap to chic. They date back to the early 1940s at the original El Rancho Vegas Hotel on the Strip. Owner Beldon Katleman dreamed up the Midnight Chuck Wagon Buffet—all you can eat for a dollar—to keep customers gambling into the wee hours. The rest is history.

Arizona Charlie's
Wild West Buffet
4575 Boulder Hwy.
(702) 951-5800
www.arizonacharlies.com

The best bet here is the breakfast with all-you-can eat pancakes, eggs, sausage, fresh juice, and bacon for under $6. Carnivores should opt for the Tuesday night steak and shrimp bar and Thursday night prime rib and potato bar to get the most flavor and bang for your buck. Slot club members get $1 off on buffet prices.

Boulder Station

Feast Gourmet Buffet
4111 Boulder Hwy.
(702) 221-2283
www.boulderstation.com

Housing more than 100 items, breakfast, lunch, and dinner buffets offer a variety for a really cheap price, especially with a slot card. In the mood for Mexican, Thai, or Chinese? You can find it all here.

Excalibur

Round Table Buffet
3850 Las Vegas Blvd. South
(877) 750-5464
www.excalibur.com

Here you can pay one price, $29.99, and have access to the buffet all day. Lots of basics like pizza, fried chicken, mac 'n' cheese, and tacos. It's not Bellagio, but for $30 for all you can eat all day on the Strip, it's a hard deal to beat.

Flamingo

Paradise Garden Buffet
3555 Las Vegas Blvd. South
(702) 733-3111
www.flamingolasvegas.com

Wrangle a seat by the window to watch the flamingos, koi ponds, and waterfalls and get a free show while you eat. International food stations at lunch and dinner feature French, German, Mexican, Italian, and Chinese specialties.

Fremont

Paradise Buffet
200 Fremont St.
(702) 385-3232
www.fremontcasino.com

Downtown
OLD Vegas
see pg. 66

Set in a tropical environment amidst a lot of fake trees, the weekend champagne brunch (around 11 bucks) is the best deal with crab legs, shrimp, prime rib, and all the regular breakfast fare as well as some Hawaiian dishes thrown in.

Gold Coast

Ports O Call Buffet
4000 West Flamingo Rd.
(702) 367-7111
www.goldcoastcasino.com

Comfort food at a very comfortable price—breakfast will run you about 6 bucks, lunch costs around $8, and you can eat dinner for under $12. Salisbury steak, BBQ, and brisket, as well as Chinese, Mexican, and Italian specialties at seven live cooking stations are all available.

Golden Nugget

Downtown old Vegas

The Buffet
129 East Fremont St.
(702) 385-7111
www.goldennugget.com

Plush booth seating and the huge seafood and salad selection and the "World Famous" bread pudding make this downtown buffet a winner. Here you can get a true taste of "Old Vegas" style food for half the price of the flashy Strip resort buffets. Lunch is a good time to go, as breakfast items are often still available.

Green Valley Ranch

Feast Around the World Buffet
2300 Paseo Verde Pkwy.
(702) 617-6831
www.greenvalleyranchresort.com

Blown glass, ceiling murals, and water accents make this buffet one of the most beautiful in the desert. Comfortable seating and a wide selection of food—Asian, Mexican, Italian, Mongolian, and American, as well as the close-to-but-not-on-the-Strip location are also pluses. Kids four and under eat free.

Harrah's

Flavors Buffet
3475 Las Vegas Blvd. South
(702) 369-5084
www.harrahslasvegas.com

Kids and folks with dietary restrictions will both be happy at this huge buffet, which offers plenty of sugar-free desserts, comfort food, and crowd-pleasing goodies including cotton candy and a huge chocolate fountain. Most hotels in the Harrah's chain offer discounts to this buffet, so ask when you check in—not like you'll need it when you can grab an all-you-can-eat meal for around 20 bucks.

Las Vegas Hilton
Hilton Buffet
3000 Paradise Rd.
(702) 732-5111
www.lvhilton.com

Really reasonable prices for the location—breakfast, lunch, or dinner won't cost you more than 18 bucks. This buffet is small compared to other resorts on the Strip but the fresh made-to-order stations, big selection of Chinese food, and free beer and wine make it worth a stop.

Main Street Station
Garden Court Buffet
200 North Main St.
(702) 387-1896
www.mainstreetcasino.com

Set in a Victorian courtyard theme, this buffet offers mainly American comfort food fare. Cheap carnivores will love the Tuesday steak night where they can hunker down on a huge T-bone and ribs for only $14.

Orleans
French Market Buffet
4500 West Tropicana Ave.
(702) 365-7111
www.orleanscasino.com

The French Market Buffet has a big selection and nice New Orleans decor without the high price tag. Don't expect beef Wellington—this buffet sticks to mostly classic American food including ribs, mac 'n' cheese, and seafood with a few live action stations offering Mexican, Italian, and Mongolian cuisine. Breakfast and Sunday BBQ rib night dinner are the best times to visit.

Plaza

Stuffed Buffet
1 Main St.
(702) 386-2110
www.plazahotelcasino.com

Loads of specialty nights—steak and crab legs Monday, southern Tuesday, all-you-can-eat ribs Thursday, seafood Friday, prime rib Saturday, and a $10 champagne brunch—keep penny pinchers lining up at this buffet. Be gloriously gluttonous without breaking your gambling budget. Players Club members get in even cheaper with $2 off entry prices.

Red Rock Resort

11011 West Charleston Blvd.
(866) 767-7773
www.redrocklasvegas.com

Low prices, high quality. It's a bit away from the Strip but worth the drive—almost Bellagio quality but for a great budget price. A mostly local clientele keeps it not too crowded and the $2 cocktails are a steal.

Rio

Carnival Buffet
3700 West Flamingo Blvd.
(866) 746-7671
www.riolasvegas.com

This huge, spacious buffet has long been a favorite of locals for the massive selection including Mexican, South American, Japanese, Chinese, Italian, and Brazilian food as well as a cool American dinner setup with fries, burgers, milkshakes, and hot dogs. The modern granite, marble, and glass decor is a nice touch and the restaurant's huge centerpiece is the dessert station with more than 70 varieties of pies, pastries, and cakes as well as a gelato station. Lots of bang for your buck. Children four through eight years of age get $7 off adult prices.

Riviera

World's Fare Buffet
2901 Las Vegas Blvd. South
(702) 734-5110
www.rivierahotel.com

The Catch No dinner buffet available, only breakfast and lunch with the buffet closing at 2 p.m.

Great for breakfast, so-so for lunch, and you're out of luck for dinner. The World's Fare Buffet offers five themed stations including Mexican, Chinese, Italian, BBQ, and Made in America as well as traditional carving stations. Use your Player's Card and it's a real deal, but breakfast or lunch will only run you a little under $12 normally.

Silverton
Seasons Buffet
3333 Blue Diamond Rd.
(702) 263-7777
www.silvertoncasino.com

The Catch Only open for brunch on Sat and Sun. Open nightly for dinner.

Specializing in Southern comfort food, the Seasons Buffet offers great food and service for the price if you can endure the often very long lines. Crab legs, prime rib, osso bucco, four different types of mimosas, and root beer floats all at $13.99 make this a good bet.

BREAKFAST **SPECIALS**

Arizona Charlie's Boulder
Sourdough Café
4575 Boulder Hwy.
(702) 951-5800
www.arizonacharliesboulder.com

This local fave serves up family-style oversized portions for meager prices including two eggs with bacon, sausage, and hash browns for about 3 bucks.

Cannery Casino Hotel
Victory Café
2121 East Craig Rd.
(702) 507-5700
www.cannerycasinos.com

This large (over 2,000 square feet) colorful café lets diners enjoy booze, prime rib, and pancakes 24/7 amidst World War II murals and memorabilia. Get up early—or stay up late—for two eggs any way, bacon or sausage, and home fries for around $2 from midnight to 7 a.m.

Eastside Cannery
Snaps
5255 North Boulder Hwy.
(702) 856-5300
www.eastsidecannery.com

Perfect for night owls, Snaps offers local fave items such as the five-alarm chili and orange chicken, as well as some of the best breakfast deals in Sin City. Two dollars will get you two eggs, bacon or sausage, hash browns and toast, or two pancakes and two pieces of bacon or sausage. Pay a little more (around $3) and get ham and eggs, hash browns, and toast, or New York steak and eggs nightly from 11 p.m. to 9 a.m.

Ellis Island
4178 Koval Lane
(702) 733-8901
www.ellisislandcasino.com

This inconspicuous space attached to a Super 8 motel a block from the Strip houses a wood-paneled super cheap coffee shop with decor featuring black and white photos of immigrants fresh off the boat from New York. Here you can get two scrambled eggs, bacon or sausage, biscuits, and gravy, for less than McDonald's! Also, order the New York steak and eggs for around $4 from 11 p.m. to 6 a.m.

JW Marriott Las Vegas
Promenade Café
221 North Rampart Blvd.
(702) 869-7777
www.marriott.com

Use your Player's Card and get a choice of six options including two eggs with bacon and toast, pancakes, or French toast all for under 2 bucks from 5 to 8 a.m. For just pennies more (around $2 and some change), you can enjoy the "Deuces Wild"—two scrambled eggs, two pieces of bacon and sausage, and two pieces of French toast—or the "Jack Stack"—four pancakes—or the biscuits and gravy special. Big spenders who are early risers can shell out a whopping $3 and some change for the "Old Vegas Breakfast" including New York steak or ham, two eggs, breakfast potatoes, and toast, offered midnight to 5 a.m.

South Point
Coronado Café
9777 Las Vegas Blvd. South
(702) 796-7111
www.southpointcasino.com

The "cabbie specials" offered after midnight and until dawn are hard to beat and include a variety of hearty breakfast items, such as two buttermilk biscuits with gravy for about $1.50, two eggs, hash browns, toast, bacon or sausage, or the pancake sandwich (a fried egg and slice of ham wrapped in a buttermilk pancake) for around $2.50; ham, steak and eggs, hash brown and toast, or a cheeseburger with fries for around 3 bucks; and New York steak and eggs with sides for around 4 bucks.

Texas Station
Yellow Rose Café
2101 Texas Star Lane
(702) 631-1000
www.texasstation.com

This country style coffee shop offers local breakfast faves for really cheap prices. If you're hankering for chow mein at 8 a.m., it is the only eatery that offers a 24-hour Chinese menu. From midnight to 6 a.m., you can get three slices of Texas toast dipped in egg and grilled with powdered sugar on top for just around $3.

STEAK **SPECIALS**

Arizona Charlie's Boulder
4575 Boulder Hwy.
(702) 951-5800
www.arizonacharliesboulder.com

This deal beats any Strip steakhouse, where prices for just the meat soar upwards of $45. At Arizona Charlie's, you can get a 14-ounce Porterhouse with fries, potato or rice, and a salad for under $11.

Ellis Island
4178 Koval Lane
(702) 733-8901
www.ellisislandcasino.com

Sink your teeth into a 10-ounce steak for just 7 bucks, complete with baked potato, green beans, bread, and a beer.

Hard Rock Hotel
Mr. Lucky's 24/7
4455 Paradise Rd.
(702) 693-5000
www.hardrockhotel.com

The steak and shrimp special known as "The Gambler's Special" isn't on the menu, so be sure to ask for it. You get an eight-ounce steak, crisp salad, three giant grilled shrimp, and a heap of mashed potatoes, all for under 8 bucks. This special is available 24 hours a day, so if you get a carnivorous craving at 4 a.m., you're still covered.

Jerry's Nugget
Jerry's Famous Coffee Shop
1821 Las Vegas Blvd. North
(702) 399-3000
www.jerrysnugget.com

For under 7 bucks, you can get surf and turf at this local favorite. The whole deal includes a choice of soup or salad, rice or potato, garlic or French bread, and four big shrimp with a steak.

Orleans

Courtyard Café
4500 West Tropicana Ave.
(702) 365-7111
www.orleanscasino.com

For those with a big appetite, the Orleans offers a 16-ounce T-bone steak dinner complete with salad and potato for just $12.99. This dish can easily be split between two friends, so your meal really comes to just $6.50.

Silverton

Sundance Grill
3333 Blue Diamond Rd.
(702) 263-7777
www.silvertoncasino.com

Another cheap surf and turf with a seven-ounce sirloin steak, a handful of fried shrimp, a baked potato or rice, and soup and salad for just $13.

Terrible's

Bougainvillea Café
4100 Paradise Rd.
(702) 733-7000
www.terriblescasinos.com

A 10 spot gets you a T-bone steak dinner plus a beer and potato at Terrible's, but it's not on the menu so you need to request it.

PRIME **RIB** SPECIALS

Arizona Charlie's Boulder

Sourdough Café
4575 Boulder Hwy.
(702) 951-5800
www.arizonacharliesboulder.com

Here you can get a surf and turf, prime rib, and four big fried shrimp, for only 8 bucks. Also included is a salad and side of veggies.

California
Market Street Café
12 Ogden St.
(800) 635-6255
www.thecal.com

The Catch Area is dangerous at night, so be sure to park in the structure and get validated at the café.

Prices at this 24-hour coffee shop are cheap, including the $8 prime rib special (yep, only $8!) with a choice of soup or salad, vegetable, potato, and dessert. Beware, there's usually a very long line. The meal also includes an all-you-can-eat salad bar. Special served from 4 to 11 p.m. daily.

Circus Circus
Casino Café
2880 Las Vegas Blvd. South
(702) 734-0410
www.circuscircus.com

Lots of comfy booths and a great prime rib deal—including a 12-ounce rib, soup or salad, vegetable, and a roll for just over 10 bucks as well as all-you-can-eat prime rib from 2 p.m. to 2 a.m. for around $12.

Ellis Island
4178 Koval Lane
(702) 733-8901
www.ellisislandcasino.com

Prime rib special includes a thick cut of meat, string beans, potato, salad, and a specialty micro-beer to boot—all for under $13.

Four Queens
Magnolia Café
202 Fremont St.
(702) 385-4011
www.fourqueens.com

Get a table overlooking the floor to keep your eyes on the casino action while eating a really cheap slab of meat. What more could a cheap gambler ask for? This dinner comes with a nice cut of beef and all the fixin's, all for under 9 bucks, served from 4 p.m. to midnight daily.

Orleans
Courtyard Café
4500 West Tropicana Ave.
(702) 365-7111
www.orleanscasino.com

This is really a deal. It includes the whole meal—10 ounces of prime rib, soup or salad, potato, rolls, dessert, and a drink all served 24 hours a day—for around 11 bucks.

South Point
Coronado Café
9777 Las Vegas Blvd. South
(866) 796-7111
www.southpointcasino.com

Thirteen bucks get you a combo of quality and convenience—a juicy prime rib, soup or salad, potato, and roll available at all times.

HOT **DOG** SPECIALS

Chicago Hot Dogs
1078 North Rancho Dr.
(702) 647-3647
www.chicagodogs.com

This authentic hot dog stand housed in an old A&W root beer joint offers all kinds of dogs (Polish, bratwurst, corndog, kosher, etc.) with all the trimmings (chili, relish, onions, tomato, sauerkraut, mustard, etc.). Their sandwiches and hamburgers are also great deals with nothing on the menu for over 6 bucks.

Circus Circus
Westside Deli
2880 Las Vegas Blvd. South
(702) 734-0410
www.circuscircus.com

Enjoy a giant foot-long half-pound dog while watching the colorful clientele at the largest permanent big top in the world. Hot dogs can be devoured for just under $3.

Eastside Cannery
The Deli
5255 North Boulder Hwy.
(702) 856-5300
www.eastsidecannery.com

Check out the deal here—not only a tasty dog but it comes with a big, tasty brew for under $2! Down a beer and a hot dog while watching the action at the sports book below.

Nathan's Hot Dogs
www.nathansfamous.com

New York New York
3790 Las Vegas Blvd. South
(702) 731-1667

Venetian Food Court
3355 Las Vegas Blvd. South
(702) 693-6212

This guilty pleasure shouldn't be missed—if you can't get to Long Island, head to Nathan's in Las Vegas, located at both ends of the Strip, for a classic New York dog. They also serve up tasty cheap cheesesteaks, burgers, and sandwiches. Go to their Web site to receive free discount coupons.

Pinks
Planet Hollywood
3667 Las Vegas Blvd. South
(702) 785-5555
www.pinkshollywood.com

This famous family-owned hot dog stand lets you try a world-famous dog that has been enjoyed by Hollywood celebs for decades. Menu items are even named after them—you can order a Kim Kardashian dog (bacon, lettuce, tomato, and guacamole), a Rosie O'Donnell dog (mustard, chili, onions, and sauerkraut), a Martha Stewart dog (relish, onions, bacon, tomato, sauerkraut, and sour cream) and even a Las Vegas Planet Hollywood dog (Polish sausage, grilled onions, mushrooms, bacon, and cheese). Good eats without the LA location's long lines, with prices starting around 3 bucks. If you get the Planet Hollywood rewards card, you can receive a 10 percent off coupon at Pinks.

Slots-O-Fun
2890 Las Vegas Blvd. South

Here you can get a huge half-pound foot-long hot dog in the dingy cedar outpost next to Circus Circus. Okay, the atmosphere ain't the Bellagio, but the dogs are big and cheap—about 2 bucks!

Suncoast
9090 Alta Dr.
(702) 636-7111
www.suncoastcasino.com

Probably the cheapest dog in Las Vegas. For less than a buck, you can get a dog at the vendor cart outside of the sports book with relish, sauerkraut, and onions. Oh, and a side of indigestion.

REALLY **CHEAP** BURGERS

California
Aloha Specialties
12 East Ogden Ave.
(702) 382-0338
www.thecal.com

It takes a while to find this restaurant located way in the back of the California casino. In addition to a long list of Hawaiian specialties, including a teriyaki burger (less than $3), you can get an old-fashioned American cheeseburger with macaroni salad for 3 bucks and change and sit down to eat it.

Fatburger
www.fatburger.com

3763 Las Vegas Blvd. South, Suite A
(702) 736-4733

4663 East Sunset Rd.
(702) 898-7200

2300 Paseo Verde Pkwy.
(702) 617-2209

1301 West Sunset Rd.
(702) 450-7820

777 West Lake Mead Pkwy.
(702) 558-9242

11011 West Charleston Blvd.
(702) 228-5744

Want to kill your hunger after a night of drinking? Here's the place. Choose from a 4-ounce, 6-ounce, 8-ounce, 16-ounce, or the XXL 24-ounce (that's three patties, in case you need to tell the doctor after your heart attack) burger that's lean on price and thick on taste. You can also get cheap chicken wings, fries, onion rings, and chili.

Fuddruckers

4195 South Grand Canyon Dr.
(702) 732-3833

6620 South Tenaya Way
(702) 478-7500

4500 West Tropicana Ave.
(702) 365-7111
www.fuddruckers.com

What's in a name? When it comes to Fuddruckers nobody knows for sure. But when you hear the name, hamburgers automatically come to mind. This self-serve burger chain lets you embellish your own burger, offered at one-third pound, half pound, three-quarter pound, and the colossal one pound, at their produce bar for a cost slightly higher than Burger King or McDonalds. If you don't like beef, they also serve tasty ostrich, buffalo, and turkey burgers.

In-N-Out

2900 West Sahara Blvd.

4888 Dean Martin Dr.

9610 West Tropicana Ave.
(800) 786-1000
www.in-n-out.com

This chain, known for their eye-catching yellow arrow logo, keeps it really simple and really cheap. The menu includes only four items—hamburger, cheeseburger, double-double, and fries. Plus some basic shakes. Service is quick, and with the drive-up window you really will be in-n-out in no time. For you cheap carb counters, you can order a flying Dutchman—two patties, two cheese, and that's it, no bun. You can also ask for a protein-style burger, which is any burger wrapped in lettuce instead of a bun. Both aren't on the menu, so you need to ask for them.

Great Burger Restaurants

Restaurants specializing in burgers have sprung up all over the Strip. Although some are triple the amount you'd pay at a fast food joint, they still are a cheap lunch or dinner in Vegas and you get the added bonus of chowing down at a classy resort restaurant instead of a sidewalk stand.

BLT Burger
The Mirage
3400 Las Vegas Blvd. South
www.bltburger.com
At fancy French chef Laurent Touronde's burger joint the traditional American sandwich gets the gourmet treatment. You can get a tasty Angus, Kobe, lamb, or turkey burger.

Burger Bar
Mandalay Bay
3930 Las Vegas Blvd. South
(702) 632-9364
www.fleurdelyssf.com
Design your own burger at master chef Hubert Keller's Burger Bar. Choose from lamb, turkey, seafood, and veggie burgers with a variety of toppings. If you get a sweet tooth or have a hankering for cocoa, you can order the chocolate burger, a donut with layers of ganache, passion fruit, and mint.

Hank's Steaks and Martinis
Green Valley Ranch
2300 Paseo Verde Pkwy.
(702) 617-7515
www.greenvalleyranchresort.com
Named for Las Vegas icon Hank Greenspun, this fancy schmancy steakhouse serves up great burgers in a romantic and classy setting.

Hash House a go go
6800 West Sahara Ave.
(702) 804-4646
www.hashhouseagogo.com

This urban meets country restaurant with metal tables and black and white photos of tractors serves up heaping helpings of everything, including the burgers. Easily split between two hungry people, it's a great deal.

Kilroy's
1021 South Buffalo Dr.
(702) 363-4933
Play Where's Waldo and try to find the Kilroy mascot that has been Photoshopped into a variety of old movie posters while enjoying one of their signature half-pounders.

Le Burger Brasserie
Paris
3655 Las Vegas Blvd. South
(877) 603-4386
www.parislasvegas.com
Another design-it-yourself burger with creative choices—the Le Paris comes with Brie, caramelized onions, and bacon. The restaurant has the ingredients of a sports bar—hot pants–wearing servers, plasma TV screens, and flair bartenders—with a much more comfortable ambiance.

The Pub
Monte Carlo
3770 Las Vegas Blvd. South
(702) 730-7777
www.montecarlo.com
This is the spot to watch your favorite sports event (huge plasma flat-screens wherever you look) while enjoying a big burger and brew. Choose from over 80 draft beers to go with your burger.

Stripburger
Fashion Show Mall
3200 Las Vegas Blvd. South
Overlook the Strip while eating your burger al fresco at the all open-air restaurant. Basic big burgers rule the menu with standard sides including fries, onion rings, pickle fries, and lots of shakes.

Tommy's Original World Famous Hamburgers
www.originaltommys.com

5208 Boulder Hwy.   3009 St. Rose Pkwy.
(702) 456-1009   (702) 644-9406

You don't need to drive to crime-ridden East LA and stand with the gang-bangers to enjoy a greasy Tommy's burger—just head to Henderson or Boulder Highway. Laden with chili, cheese, and the rest of the toppings, it's not pretty to look at but it tastes damn good. Note that all burgers are served with tomato, onion, pickle, mustard, and chili, so if you don't want any of those ingredients be sure to tell them when you order.

HAPPY **HOURS**

Fortunately for all of us cheap drinkers, there has been an explosion of happy hours in Sin City recently as restaurants hit hard by the depressing recession try to find new and better ways to lure in customers. To some, the words "happy hour" conjure an image less than ecstatic—a group of men hunkered over two-for-one domestic drafts, making periodic trips to a steam table offering complimentary Swedish meatballs and cocktail franks. But in Vegas, where the cost of an evening out seems to keep rising, happy hour often becomes one of the cheap bastard's primary nightlife options offering gourmet appetizers, brews, and cocktails at budget prices.

The Back Door Lounge
1415 East Charleston Blvd.
(702) 385-2018
Weekdays 5 to 7 p.m., $2 beer and well drinks

This gay bar is a nice loud place for some brews and chat with a low-pressure atmosphere and fair drink prices. Weekends heat up with Friday and Saturday night disco parties and midnight drag shows.

Ballpark Lounge
7380 South Eastern Ave., Suite 101
(702) 361-1961
Daily 2 to 6 p.m., $1.25 drafts, $4 pitchers, $1.75 wells

If you've got a case of spring training fever, check out the Ballpark Lounge, where you can find America's two favorite pastimes—baseball and beer.

Big Dog's Cafe & Casino
6390 West Sahara Ave.
(702) 876-3647
www.bigdogsbrews.com
Thursdays $2 off all Big Dog brews, $8 off Big Dog brew pitchers

Drink doggy style at this dog-themed bar with murals of puppies, paw prints, and canine paraphernalia. They make some of the best sets of brew in town, from tasty hefeweizens to thick stouts that are worth barking about.

Blondies Sports Bar and Grill
3663 Las Vegas Blvd. South
(702) 737-0444
www.blondieslasvegas.com
Daily 3 to 6 p.m., $20 gets you all you can drink

Centrally located in the Miracle Mile shops at Planet Hollywood, this rowdy sports bar is perfect for Nicholas Cage *Leaving Las Vegas* types who just want to drink as much as possible, all for just $20.

Blue Martini
Town Square
6593 Las Vegas Blvd., Suite 214
(702) 949-2583
www.bluemartinilounge.com
Daily 4 to 8 p.m., half off drinks and appetizers; Wed ladies get a free drink after 8 p.m.

Enjoy live music and a huge choice (34) of large martinis at this popular locals watering hole featuring four bars and an outdoor patio.

Bootlegger Bistro
7700 Las Vegas Blvd. South
(702) 736-4939
www.bootleggerlasvegas.com
Weekdays 3 to 6 p.m., $1.50 domestic drafts, $3 house wine

This longtime south Strip gem exudes old-school swank and low-key elegance with Vegas memorabilia plastered everywhere, dim lighting, and atmosphere straight out of the movie set of *Swingers*. Lounge lizards and Strip professionals crowd the place for impromptu jams so you can hear some great free music while enjoying the happy hour.

Carmine's Little Italy/Instant Replay
2940 South Durango Dr.
(702) 243-7777
www.lvcarmines.com
Wed 3 to 10 p.m., $3 martinis

At this raucous sports bar you name the sport and they watch it here on dozens of big screen TVs. Food portions are huge, so cheap sports fans can easily share an entrée after downing drinks during happy hour.

Casa Di Amore
2850 East Tropicana Ave.
(702) 433-4967
www.casidiamore.com
Daily 4 to 6 p.m., $1 off drinks

Looking to find the real Sopranos? They are probably hanging out at Casa Di Amore, a cozy Italian-American cocktail lounge where you're much more likely to eat the fishes than sleep with them.

Champagne's Café
3557 South Maryland Pkwy.
(702) 737-1699
www.champagnescafe.blogspot.com
Daily 2 a.m. to noon, $1.25 drafts and house wine, $1.50 well drinks, Schnapps, and red drafts, $2 bloody Marys; Sun and Mon, all-day happy hour, most drinks $1.50; Tues is all-day ladies happy hour, most drinks $1 for ladies.

This dark, intimate, and a bit seedy throwback to old Las Vegas is one of the few free-standing bars in town. It draws a hipster crowd who like the jukebox full of Sinatra tunes and the simple fact that basically this is a joint to drink and converse.

Champs Lounge
3603 Las Vegas Blvd. North
(702) 644-8321
Daily 3 to 6 p.m., $1.50 domestics, two-for-one drafts, $1.25 well drinks

If you've got a hankering to belt out some karaoke—and after a few drinks, don't we all?—Champs is a great place to do it. The quarter pool tables complement the cheap drink menu.

Coyote Ugly
3790 Las Vegas Blvd. South
(702) 740-3660
www.coyoteuglysaloon.com
Sun to Thurs 6 to 8 p.m., no cover, two-for-one drinks

Coyote Ugly was one of the worst films of 2000, but fortunately the bar Coyote Ugly is a lot more interesting. It maintains the movie's signature bar-dancing and throws in some good drink specials.

Crown & Anchor British Pub
1350 East Tropicana Ave.
(702) 739-8676
www.crownandanchorlv.com
Daily 3 to 6 p.m., $1 off all imports

The Crown & Anchor is the place to go if you want a huge selection of brews to choose from in a real pub atmosphere with wooden accents and British memorabilia inside and an adjacent outdoor patio.

Double Down Saloon
4640 Paradise Rd.
(702) 791-5775
www.doubledownsaloon.com
Weekdays 10 a.m. to 6 p.m., $2 domestics, $3 well drinks

Lots of UNLV students, rotating bands, and strong drinks with innovative names characterize this small watering hole. Oh, don't forget the house rule: You puke, you clean.

Firefly
3900 Paradise Rd.
(702) 369-3971
www.fireflylv.com
Daily 3 to 6 p.m., half price drinks and complimentary tapas

This tapas kitchen and bar is a favorite of locals, where loungers can listen to live music, enjoy some fine Spanish small fusion meals, and get half-price drinks and free tapas during happy hour.

Freakin' Frog
4700 South Maryland Pkwy. Unit 8
(702) 597-9702
www.freakinfrog.com
Mon to Sat, 2 to 6 p.m., rotating beer specials

No glitz or glamour here, just lots of beer choices—so many it's freakin' ridiculous. Located across from UNLV, this pub style bar attracts students and serious drinkers. The upstairs whiskey bar offers a massive whiskey and scotch selection. Freakin' Frog is smoke free, so you can wear your nice clothes here without leaving and smelling like an ashtray.

Gordon Biersch
3987 Paradise Rd.
(702) 312-5247
www.gordonbiersch.com
Weekdays 4 to 6:30 p.m., $4.95 appetizers, $1 off Gordon Biersch's special lagers and $5 martinis

Located a few minutes off of the Strip, Gordon Biersch is a microbrewery chain in classic pub style offering an extensive happy hour with tasty appetizers such as Southwest egg rolls, chicken wings, garlic fries, sliders, and mini pizzas, and a wide selection of beers.

Hofbräuhaus
Also small gift shop see pg. 23
4510 Paradise Rd.
(702) 853-2337
www.hofbrauhauslasvegas.com
Sun to Thurs 4 to 6 p.m., 20 percent off bar tab

In addition to serving up an impressive selection of wursts, schnitzels, bratens, and strudels, the Hofbrauhaus has tasty ales and lagers imported directly from Bavaria. Check out the indoor beer garden, a nice place to guzzle down a few liters of the golden delicious. During happy hour they also offer a free pretzel, so ask for it!

Ice House Lounge

650 South Main St.
(702) 315-2570
www.icehouselounge.com
Daily 4 to 7 p.m.: $2 domestics, $2 wells

The retro-chic Ice House has quickly become a favorite of hipsters and yuppies with its art deco design, '60s style furniture, and black and white mob photos.

J.C. Wooloughan

221 North Rampart Blvd.
(702) 869-7777
Weekdays 4 to 7 p.m., all beers, wine and well drinks discounted; Thurs nights from 9 p.m. to midnight drinks are $1 for ladies

Irish expat J. C. Wooloughan brought a boatload of paraphernalia from his favorite Dublin drinking spots to create this authentic self-named pub. In addition to offering a good happy hour and great atmosphere, Wooloughan's also broadcasts English football games (that's soccer to us).

Kopper Keg

2257 South Rainbow Blvd.
(702) 254-4299
Weekdays 2 to 6 p.m., $1.75 domestic beers, $1.50 drafts, $1.75 well drinks

The Kopper Keg's drink menu is large, reasonably priced, and the draft selection includes Foster's ($1.75) and Newcastle ($2.50), while the bottled stuff dips as low as $1.25 during happy hour. During football games, all drafts are a buck. Now that's cheap!

Magoo's

5765 West Tropicana Ave.
(702) 368-1515

2585 Flamingo Rd.
(702) 732-1515

3234 North Decatur Blvd.
(702) 631-7708
Daily 3 to 6 p.m., $1 domestic drafts, $2 domestic bottles, $2.75 wells

Even the near-sighted cartoon figure Mr. Magoo could see the virtue of Magoo's, with three laid-back joints throughout Las Vegas. Each location has darts, video poker gambling at the bar, pool tables, and some cheap drinks.

Drinking for Next to Nothing in the Casinos

The main rule of thumb for drinking on the cheap in Las Vegas is not to order any alcohol from the bars or restaurants in the casinos. You can get almost free drinks at the slots or tables while you are chasing that dream of the one big quit–your-job-sized win.

Unfortunately, there's no such thing as a totally free drink in Las Vegas. Really cheap, yes, but all out free, no. Sure, every casino sends their cocktail waitresses around to take your orders, but if you aren't dropping money into a machine (that will cost you some quarters at least) you won't get a drink offer and if you have any hope of seeing the waitress again you need to tip. The trick to drinking cheap in casinos is to tip well—if you are playing the 25 cent slots, tip your waitress $2 and she'll be back by the time your next drink needs to be ordered. After that, $1 per drink is fine.

Origin India

4480 Paradise Rd.
(702) 734-6342
www.originindiarestaurant.com
Weekdays 4 to 7 p.m., half-priced appetizers and specialty martinis and mojitos

Here you can get a great Indian dinner and a drink to boot at a bargain price during their happy hour. Most entrees, such as tasty lamb kebobs and samosas fall from $9 to $4.50 from 4 to 7 p.m.

Paymon's Mediterranean Café and Hookah Lounge

4147 South Maryland Pkwy.
(702) 731-6030

8380 West Sahara Ave.
(702) 731-6030
www.paymons.com

Tues 5 p.m. to 1 a.m., half price hummus, baba ghanoush, pizzas, and appetizers, $1.75 domestic beers, $2 imported bottles, $4 well drinks

Get your hookah and hummus fix while lounging in the red velvet luxury of Paymon's Mediterranean Café and Hookah Lounge and enjoy the happy hour specials. The food here is pretty tasty too and the portions are huge, so take a friend and split a good cheap dinner while enjoying the drink specials.

Pogo's Tavern
2103 North Decatur Blvd.
(702) 646-9735
Weekdays 2:30 to 5:30, $1 drafts, $1.75 well drinks, 25 cents off call drinks

This west side bar, a favorite of locals, is best known for its Friday night live jazz jams, which draw formidable players who once supplied music for Strip productions. In addition to the cool music, the vibe and atmosphere are laid back with cozy booths and dark wood paneling.

Roy's Restaurant
620 East Flamingo Rd.
(702) 691-2053

8701 West Charleston Blvd.
(702) 838-3620
www.roysrestaurant.com
Weekdays 4:30 to 7 p.m., $5 appetizers and beverages

Get in the aloha spirit at Roy's, the popular upscale Hawaiian chain restaurant serving up tasty Japanese, Hawaiian, and French fusion fare.

The Rum Runner
1801 East Tropicana Ave.
(702) 736-6366

3726 East Flamingo Rd.
(702) 434-5019

3050 Desert Inn Rd.
(702) 732-7373
www.rumrunnervegas.com
$1.75 drafts weekdays from 5 to 8 p.m.

The Rum Runner has it all—three locations, darts, video poker, shuffleboard, a jukebox, and cheap draft beers.

Sand Dollar Blues Lounge
3355 Spring Mountain Rd.
(702) 871-6651
www.sanddollarblues.com
$2 Bud, Bud Light drafts weekdays from 5 to 8 p.m.

Just up the road from Treasure Island, this small, smoky bar is one of the Vegas's premier blues spots, hosting hot regional acts as well as local faves. The Sand Dollar is the place to go when you're tired of getting the once-over one too many times at the hipper Strip nightspots.

Steiner's Pub
1750 North Buffalo Dr.
(888) 531-1739

8168 Las Vegas Blvd. South
(702) 214-6700
www.steinerspub.com
Weekdays 4 to 7 p.m., $1 Pucker shots, $1.75 domestic bottles, $2 domestic pints, $2 Long Islands, $2.25 import micro bottles, $2.50 premium well drinks, $2.75 import micro pints; Weekends 9 a.m. to 4 p.m., $2 domestic drafts, $2.50 Absolut Bloody Marys, $2.50 Cuervo margaritas, $4.99 wings, brats, and Phillies.

The Catch Both locations do not observe the no smoking law, so if you venture inside, by the time you exit expect to smell like an ashtray.

Both Steiner's locations share the same cool interior full of historic memorabilia, video poker, and the same massive selection of brews with over 30 beers available on tap. They've got hefeweizens, stouts, bocks, and ales from a variety of Vegas breweries.

Thirstbusters
697 North Valle Verde Dr.
(702) 454-9200
Weekdays 3 to 6 p.m., $1.50 drafts, $1.25 wells, $1.25 house wines; daily 1 a.m. to 9 a.m, $1 drafts, $1 wells

Thirstbusters serves up over 120 different beers including everything from Kirin Ichiban to Pilsner Urquell. Join their "Beer Battalion" by imbibing all 120 beers in 365 days or less.

The Tilted Kilt
3700 West Flamingo Rd.
(702) 777-2463
Daily 4 to 6 p.m., $2 domestics, $3 imports or premiums

This franchise of the national Scotch-Irish-American alehouse chain is housed inside the Rio. If you're thirsty for cheap drinks and free entertainment, you can grab any of its 24 draft brews and watch the Carnaval-inspired Masquerade Village right outside of the bar's doors.

JUST **PLAIN** CHEAP **DRINKS**

Cheers
1220 East Harmon Ave.
(702) 734-2454
$4 22-ounce Newcastle and Bass drafts

Not necessarily the bar where everyone knows your name and you won't find Norm, Carla, or Sam hanging around, but it's a good place to get a big cheap beer.

Dew Drop Inn
4200 Boulder Hwy.
(702) 458-3184
$1 16-ounce drafts during all NASCAR races

This country-western bar attracts local thirsty construction workers. The sign next to the front door reads "Welcome, you are a stranger here but once." Locals frequent this neighborhood bar for their great beer prices and friendly atmosphere.

Dino's
1516 Las Vegas Blvd. South
(702) 382-3894
www.dinoslv.com
$7 62-ounce domestic pitchers

Dino's is the ideal spot to grab a pitcher and bust a few rounds of karaoke with karaoke king Danny G. It's also a great place to throw back a few cheap cocktails or Buds.

Four Kegs
276 North Jones Blvd.
(702) 870-0255
www.four-kegs.com
$1.75 domestic drafts

This longtime locals joint has become crowded due to being featured on the Food Network's *Diners, Drive-Ins and Dives,* but is still worth a visit for their killer stromboli and good happy hour prices. If you need a stromboli fix at 3 a.m., you are covered—this dive stays open 24 hours.

Four Mile Bar
3650 Boulder Hwy.
(702) 431-6936
$1.75 15-ounce draft, $2 wells, $5.25 domestic pitchers

The Four Mile Bar is an urban, retro cowboy dive along Boulder Highway with cheap drinks and pitchers.

Hurricane Harry's
3190 West Sahara Ave.
(702) 253-6013
$7 48-ounce domestic beers

Half bar, half old-school nightclub, Hurricane Harry's serves drinks on its seven outdoor patios, where extra-large margaritas made with one of the bar's 40 tequilas will ensure a wild night.

The Lift
3045 South Valley View Blvd.
(702) 364-0306
$1 drafts daily from 5 to 7 p.m.

Join the local construction crews who hang out each afternoon at this funky midtown bar, which houses video poker machines, plenty of flat-screens to watch the latest game, and tables in addition to bar seating.

CHEAP **CUPS** OF **JOE**

If you want a quick jolt of caffeine to wake you out of a gambling or hangover haze, there is always a big chain (think Starbucks, Coffee Bean and Tea Leaf, Seattle's Best Coffee, It's A Grind, etc.) somewhere near the casino floor at all of the hotels and resorts as well as multiple locations throughout Las Vegas.

But if you desire a welcoming oasis from the Starbucked world, there are a number of good bean roasting sites in Sin City. The best non-chain coffeehouses offer a refuge from the bright lights and sounds of the Strip where java lovers can relax in a place with a neighborhood feel and have the opportunity to chat with fellow connoisseurs of mochaccinos and lattes, or conversely bury their heads in a good book.

Bouchon Coffee Stand
Venetian
3355 Las Vegas Blvd. South
(702) 414-6203
www.venetian.com

Located near the Phantom Theater in the Venetian, this small and much cheaper outpost of the larger Thomas Keller famed restaurant offers amazing pastries and macaroons that pair perfectly with the freshly brewed java. Grab a cuppa and a few tasty goodies and head over the watch the gondolas drift by.

Brewed Awakening
2305 East Sahara Ave., Suite F
(702) 457-7050

This European-style coffee house offers strong cups of coffee in an intimate setting. Paintings from local artists adorn the walls, which adds to the neighborhood laid-back vibe. Local musicians provide free live music on Saturday and Sunday.

Espressamente Illy
Palazzo
3325 Las Vegas Blvd. South
(702) 869-2233
www.palazzolasvegas.com

Enjoy a perfectly brewed espresso at the Espressamente Illy coffee bar for less than your local Starbucks. This modern Italian café has bright red walls, black and chrome tables and chairs, and an abundance of paninis, soups, salads, fresh crepes, pastries and 54 flavors of gelato to indulge in along with your imported cup of joe. Grab a seat by the window to people-watch and view the three-story waterfall and reflecting pools in the Palazzo's octagonal domed atrium.

Espresso Culture and Cuisine
9555 South Eastern Ave.
(702) 243-4559
www.espressoculturelv.com

Serving up hot cups of Illy off the Strip, Espresso Culture and Cuisine is a local fave offering a chill vibe, modern stylish decor, and great Italian paninis and pastries. They also serve wine and a large variety of teas for those foregoing the caffeine. Free games and books provide entertainment while you sip your brew of choice.

Greenwich Village Coffee Company
3790 Las Vegas Blvd. South
(702) 740-6969

Looking for an east coast bagel to go with your cup of joe? Head to Greenwich Village Coffee Company in New York New York resort where you can get a toasted bagel, pastry, donut, or muffin to go with an espresso and help cure a hangover without breaking the bank—donuts go for just a buck.

Lollicup Coffee and Tea
6605 Las Vegas Blvd. South, Suite 234
(702) 260-8988
www.lollicup.com

If boba is your beverage of choice, head to Lollicup in Town Square. In addition to a large variety of bobas, they offer more than 150 different types of drinks including milk teas, flavored teas, smoothies, slushes, juices, and coffees. Sign up for their VIP card and get 20 percent off drinks and 10 percent off snacks.

Rejavanate

3300 East Flamingo Rd., #23
(702) 433-3304
www.rejavanatecoffee.com

Rejavanate has it all—free Wi-Fi, great snacks, lots of comfy seating, and a variety of tasty coffee drinks. Live local bands often play on weekends with no cover charge.

Roasted Bean

3400 Las Vegas Blvd. South

739 Las Vegas Blvd. South
(702) 791-7111

If you are in need of a caffeine and sugar fix, the Roasted Bean is your spot. Offering huge portions of pies (around $5), pastries (under $4), and cupcakes ($2) which can all be split between two people, this small coffee bar offers a nice refuge from the casino action at the Mirage and Aria.

Sunrise Coffee Company

3130 East Sunset Rd., Suite A
(702) 433-3304
www.sunrisecoffeelv.com

Vegans and eco-friendly coffee drinkers are big fans of this quaint indie coffee house, where organic beans are roasted locally. Free Wi-Fi, nice patio seating, and a large variety of vegetarian options are also pluses. Sunrise uses all compost-friendly cups so their coffees and teas are tasty and they don't hurt the environment. Ed Begley would be proud.

HAIR, BEAUTY, AND MASSAGE:
FREESTYLE

*"Everyone should have enough money
to get plastic surgery."*
—BEVERLY JOHNSON

How much of your "personal appearance" budget goes to hair and beauty care? More likely than not, those cuts, massages, and make-up applications—not to mention products and equipment—are second only to clothing in looking-good costs. If you're penny pinching or just looking for a bit of adventure, there are several options to the normal salon or spa appointment with its heady price tag.

One of the best ways to save on hair care, at least on cuts, is to ask if your salon includes in-between trims as part of its service. Rather than pay for more overall cuts than you really need, bangs or stray hairs can probably be cleaned up at no charge.

Beauty and massage therapy schools and colleges are also a great way to save cash. Most have student clinics that offer drastically reduced prices due to the fact that a student is providing the services. This usually takes quite a bit longer as an instructor constantly needs to check the work, but the end result is usually good and at a quarter of the price of a Strip salon or spa.

BEAUTY **SCHOOL** DEALS **AND** DISCOUNTS

Academy of Hair Design
5191 West Charleston Blvd. #150
(702) 878-1185
www.advegas.com

This 11,500-square-foot campus offers reduced rates on skin and hair services. You'll spend more time in the chair because students are relatively new to providing cuts and facials, but the savings are well worth it. You can walk out with a new do and mani/pedi for under $50!

Aveda Institute Las Vegas
4856 South Eastern Ave.
(702) 459-2900
www.avedalasvegas.com

You literally can spend all day here getting a treatment but you will only pay a small amount for a professional cut, color, or manicure. This large facility offers facials, cuts, colors, and nail treatments. Every cut—they start at $15— also gets a complimentary mini-facial, scalp massage, and hand massage.

G Skin and Beauty Institute
2585 East Flamingo Rd., Suites 5 to 8
(702) 953-9695
www.gbeautyschools.com

Sure, you are going to have to let a student near your noggin and tootsies with scissors and other sharp instruments, but for these cheap prices—a haircut will only cost you around 5 or 6 bucks—get over it. You can get waxed, buffed, and coiffed for a quarter of what you would pay elsewhere.

Paul Mitchell Las Vegas
9490 South Eastern Ave., Suite 100
(702) 740-4247
www.pmtslasvegas.com

This bustling salon located in a small strip mall offers clients cuts, colors, waxes, make-up application and nail treatments. Basic prices are low, but for even better discounts, check their Web site.

MASSAGE AND BODY WORK

European Massage Therapy School
8751 West Charleston Blvd., Suite 295
(702) 202-2455
www.school-for-massage.com

Close to Summerlin, this school offers deep tissue, reflexology, and shiatsu in addition to traditional treatments. You won't find a steam room or Jacuzzi, but for $25 you'll get a good massage for 50 minutes. An extra $15 gets you another relaxing half hour.

High Tech Institute
2320 South Rancho Dr.
(866) 385-6700
www.hightechinstitute.edu

Visit the massage therapy clinic and get your choice of treatments including Swedish, hot stone, deep tissue, and shiatsu for $25. If you know a current student you can score an even better deal—only $15 for a one-hour massage.

Nevada School of Massage Therapy
2381 East Windmill Lane, Suite 4
(702) 456-4325
www.nevadasmt.com

The Catch Appointments are walk-in only so you might have to wait a bit for your rub-down.

If you are in need of a good rub-down but find yourself short on funds, the Nevada School of Massage Therapy offers Swedish, shiatsu, sports-therapy, and a variety of other treatments all for under $35. It's only open Saturday and Sunday from 8 a.m. to 5:30 p.m.

NO-**COST** MAKEOVERS

Many department store and retail make-up stores are filled with artists ready to give you a new look for free. The expectation is that you will purchase a product when your transformation is complete, but you aren't required to buy anything. Even if you leave with just a gloss, it will cost a fraction of the cost of a make-up application at a spa or resort. Here are places where you can sample the goods and even get help applying them for nothing (or next to nothing).

Fashion Show Mall

Bloomingdales
Dillards
Macy's
Nordstrom
3200 Las Vegas Blvd. South
(702) 784-7000
www.thefashionshow.com

You can visit all of these chain department stores in one stop at the Fashion Show Mall. They are also located throughout the city and all offer dozens of make-up counters where you can get gussied up for free. Many counters also offer promotions where if you buy a certain dollar amount of product (usually around $25) you can get a bag of free products including lipsticks, rouge, and mascara as a gift.

MAC

3500 Las Vegas Blvd. South
(702) 369-8770

3700 South Maryland Pkwy.
(702) 696-1733

6639 Las Vegas Blvd. South
(702) 492-1173
www.maccosmetics.com

The Catch Most full-on make-up applications require an appointment in advance and some locations require that guests purchase a set dollar amount of product. Usually the requirement is only $25, so for the price of a new foundation bottle you can leave looking like a star.

This trendy upscale make-up store specializes in variety with hundreds of eye shadow and lip shades ranging from fuchsia to turquoise. They also carry makeup tools, skin care, foundation, and accessories for fashion forward clients to color their world.

Sephora

3377 Las Vegas Blvd. South
(702) 735-3896

3663 Las Vegas Blvd. South
(702) 737-0550

6671 Las Vegas Blvd. South
(702) 361-3727
www.sephora.com

Sephora is similar to an emporium of beauty aids. Neatly organized shelves present the latest in fragrances, make-up, and skin care products. The French company offers over 150 products with employees dressed in all black ready to assist customers with free samples and applications.

GETTING HITCHED:
ON THE CHEAP

*"I think men who have a pierced ear
are better prepared for marriage.
They've experienced pain and bought jewelry."*
—RITA RUDNER

Some come to Vegas to get rich quick and others come to get hitched quick. It happens once every five minutes. With just two words, people's lives are changed forever. No, the words aren't "You win." Rather, the magic phrase that rings out with Swiss-movement regularity is "I do." In Sin City, getting married can be nearly as uncomplicated as going through a drive-up window at a fast food restaurant. Quick, easy, and cheap. For thousands of couples who tie the knot here, that makes for a very happy marriage.

Justifiably the wedding capital of the world, it's pretty easy to get married in Sin City. Just ask Britney. First find your mate. Then head to the Clark County Marriage License Bureau (201 Clark Ave., open 8 a.m. to midnight daily) to get your license (which costs $55, and you need to pay in cash, traveler's check, or cashier's check). Bring proof of age (driver's license, passport, or birth certificate will do), your social security number, and parental consent if you are under eighteen. No blood test or waiting period is needed. Off to the chapel you go!

Nearly every major hotel on the Strip has a wedding chapel and offers unique or traditional opportunities to tie the proverbial knot. But for a ceremony on the cheap, one of the many Vegas downtown wedding chapels is a good bet.

The Cheapest Option

Head to the Office of Civil Marriages and have your ceremony executed by a Commissioner of Civil Marriages for a mere $50. Open daily from 8 a.m. to 10 p.m.; you just need a witness and a few "I do's". No muss, no fuss. If you don't bring a witness, most other couples waiting will be happy to stand in as your witness if you return the favor.

CHEAP **CHAPELS**

A Chapel by the Courthouse
201 East Bridger Ave.
(702) 384-9099
www.achapelbythecourthouse.com
Daily 8 a.m. to midnight

This chapel is probably the most convenient as the name says it all. Located downtown within walking distance from the marriage license bureau, this very small chapel will provide a quickie wedding for just $40. The interior is a big lounge with red velvet seats and mauve carpets, but for 40 bucks, what do you expect?

Chapel of Love
1430 Las Vegas Blvd. South
(702) 387-0155
www.vegaschapeloflove.com
Daily 10 a.m. to 8 p.m.

What used to be the site of a Bob's Big Boy restaurant in the 1960s is today the Chapel of Love. It houses a variety of themed kitschy rooms to tie the knot including a Renaissance Fantasy Chapel where you can dress up, a Garden Chapel with a fountain and rainbows, a Lover's Pathway with lots of flowers, and the Short and Sweet which seats just 12 guests. Oh, and there's the drive-up window where you can say "I do" without leaving your car. Sure, it's amidst gentlemen's clubs and psychic readers, but hey, it's Vegas. Costs range from $50 up to $1,000.

Chapel of the Bells
2233 Las Vegas Blvd. South
(702) 735-6803
www.chapelofthebellslasvegas.com
9 a.m. to 10 p.m. Sun through Thurs, open till 1 a.m. Fri and Sat

Offering ceremonies ranging from intimate to grand, this Sin City chapel has been around for over 50 years. It's clean (ivory drapes, white chairs and altar) and famous—with a cameo in several Hollywood films including *Honeymoon in Vegas*, *Indecent Proposal*, and *Vegas Vacation*. Celebs who tied the knot here include Mickey Rooney and Kelly Ripa. You can get a basic package for just over $100 or go all out for $400.

Graceland Wedding Chapel
610 Las Vegas Blvd. South
(702) 474-6655
www.gracelandchapel.com
9 a.m. to midnight Sun through Thurs, open till 3 a.m. Fri and Sat

If you want to get married by Elvis, here is the spot. This cute white chapel with blue trim is cozy and basic, but pretty inside. When you enter you can see all the pics of celebrities who got hitched here—Jon Bon Jovi, etc.—and you might recognize the chapel from the movie *When Fools Rush In*. Some of the best Elvis impersonators perform ceremonies here, including Brendon Paul who is a dead ringer visually and vocally for the King. Elvis packages include your choice of Blue Hawaii Elvis, Gold Lamé Elvis, Jumpsuit Elvis, or even dueling Elvises. That's right, both young and old versions. Only in Vegas. Elvis ceremonies from $199 to $800.

A Hollywood Wedding Chapel
2207 Las Vegas Blvd. South
(702) 795-8119
www.ahollywoodweddingchapel.com
Daily 11 a.m. to 8 p.m.

Once the home of the Red Fez, a popular nightclub and hangout for the Rat Pack, the current Hollywood connection ends with celebrity pictures and movie posters along the narrow hallway. The small chapel holds up to 40 guests and will dispense a quick marriage at a low cost. Packages begin at $99.

Little Chapel of the Flowers
1717 Las Vegas Blvd. South
(702) 735-4331
www.littlechapel.com
9 a.m. to 9 p.m. Mon through Sat

Probably housing the prettiest decor of any free-standing chapel in Vegas, this famous chapel is family owned and features several chapels to accommodate different size parties and tastes. The small 20-seat Magnolia Chapel is quaint, the Victorian 30-seat is a bit larger and decorated in light browns, and the larger La Capella Italian-themed chapel can fit 70 guests. The lovely outside

Celebrity Weddings in Las Vegas

Las Vegas has been the site of many celebrity unions. Some survived the test of time and others survived two days of headlines and blew away like the sands of the Nevada desert. Here are some of Sin City's most famous love knots.

The "I Do's"

Paul Newman and Joanne Woodward: The couple tied the knot on January 1958, at the now defunct El Rancho Hotel/Casino. Their marriage was as successful and classy as their careers.

Betty White and Allen Ludden: Golden Girl Betty White married the game show host in 1963 and they remained true until his sudden death in 1981.

Steve Lawrence and Eydie Gorme: This famous singing duo tied the knot at the home of Beldon Katelman in Las Vegas in 1957. The couple continued to perform on the Strip for years.

Ann-Margret and Roger Smith: The screen sex kitten wed actor Roger Smith at the Riviera Hotel in May 1967. They have remained a devoted couple through thick and thin.

Robert Goulet and Vera Chochorovska Novak: The actor-singer wed the glamorous Macedonian-born public relations exec in 1982. More than 1,200 guests attended the reception at the legendary Dunes.

Michael Caine and Shakira Baksh: The *Alfie* actor found love at first sight (through a Maxwell House coffee TV ad) with model Shakira Baksh and they wed at the Candlelight Wedding Chapel in 1973 and have been going strong ever since.

Kirk Douglas and Anne Buydens: After meeting on a Paris film set, the actors flew to Sin City to get hitched at the Sahara Hotel.

Jon Bon Jovi and Dorothea Hurley: The uber-rocker wed his high school sweetheart at the Graceland Wedding Chapel in April 1989.

Clint Eastwood and Dina Ruiz: Wed in Steve Wynn's Shadow Creek home, Dirty Harry planned a surprise wedding for his newscaster fiancé.

Mark Consuelos and Kelly Ripa: The soap opera stars (*All My Children*) got hitched in May 1996 at the Chapel of the Bells.

Kevin Dillon and Jane Stuart: The *Entourage* star couldn't resist getting married by an Elvis impersonator. Now the couple has one child.

The "I Don'ts"

Mickey Rooney and Ava Gardner: Rooney began his love affair with Las Vegas weddings with the gorgeous Gardner on Jan. 10, 1942. Two years and one divorce later, he was back for his second of what would eventually be seven more trips down the aisle of the Little Chapel of the West.

Frank Sinatra and Mia Farrow: Ol' Blue Eyes wed his pixieish child bride on July 19, 1966, at the Sands, baby. Two years later, he served her with divorce papers on the set of *Rosemary's Baby*. Hell hath no fury like a crooner scorned.

Elvis Presley and Priscilla Beaulieu: Just one week prior to the wedding of his sultry *Viva Las Vegas* co-star (see Ann-Margret among the "I Do's"), the King married his girlish 'Cilla during a 3:30 a.m., eight-minute ceremony at the Aladdin Hotel on May 1, 1967. The marriage lasted six years. The hotel was imploded.

Cary Grant and Dyan Cannon: The debonair actor married a much younger Cannon at the Dunes hotel and the two were divorced a year and a half later.

Elizabeth Taylor and Eddie Fisher: The day crooner Fisher received his divorce papers from Debbie Reynolds, he headed to the chapel with Liz. The marriage only lasted a few years.

George Hamilton and Alana Collins: They tied the knot in October 1972 at the Las Vegas Hilton. Hamilton's tan survived longer than their vows.

Bruce Willis and Demi Moore: Married in their suite at the Golden Nugget in downtown Las Vegas in 1987, this marriage lasted longer than most in Hollywood, ending in divorce a decade later.

Angelina Jolie and Billy Bob Thornton: Before becoming a major star and half of Brangelina, the actress married Billy Bob Thornton (his fifth marriage) at the Little Church of the West. The marriage ended in divorce after three years.

Britney Spears and Jason Alexander: The pop star wed a high school friend at the Little White Chapel in early 2004. One of the shortest celeb Vegas weddings in history, the nuptials were annulled two days later.

garden area can seat 35 for ceremonies under the stars. Service here is serious and the staff makes sure everything is taken care of. The small garden with a bridge and waterfall is perfect for pictures. If you want a more traditional wedding with different packages this is a good choice. Intimate simple ceremonies begin at $195 but can go up to $10,000 for extremely decadent packages.

Little Church of the West
4617 Las Vegas Blvd. South
(702) 739-7971
www.littlechurchlv.com
Daily 8 a.m. to midnight

This rustic charming historic chapel was founded in 1942 and was originally part of the Western theme park of the Frontier Hotel. It's a replica of a California mining town 1849 church, complete with redwood interior walls, wood floors, ceiling beams and shingled roof. A fave of celebs including Angelina Jolie and Billie Bob Thornton as well as Richard Gere and Cindy Crawford, it can get a bit noisy as it's located between Las Vegas Boulevard and McCarran Airport. Packages start at $199.

Little White Wedding Chapel
1301 Las Vegas Blvd. South
(702) 382-5943
www.littlewhitechapel.com
Open 24 hours

Brittany, Sinatra, Michael Jordan, and Bruce and Demi all took vows at this busy and famous chapel. Housing Sin City's first drive-thru chapel, there are five chapel choices ranging from intimate (12 people) to very large (80). They also offer a drive-thru window, the "Tunnel of Vows," under an elaborate carport for $50. Packages start at $199.

Mon Bel Ami Wedding Chapel
607 Las Vegas Blvd. South
(702) 378-4445
www.monbelami.com
10 a.m. to midnight weekdays, open till 3 a.m. on Fri and Sat

The Catch Read all of the contract carefully as the chapel does not allow you to bring in your own flowers or take any pictures on the grounds (you have to hire their photographer).

Located a few blocks from Fremont Street, this newer pretty chapel is decorated in gold and honey with green and rose accents. A few years back it replaced the tired and weathered Silver Bell Wedding Chapel with a completely new structure including a gazebo and an outside yard. Packages here start at $199. Weddings are booked an hour apart, which is rare for Vegas chapels, so couples can relax and not be rushed through their nuptials.

San Francisco Sally's Victorian Chapel
1394 Las Vegas Blvd. South
(702) 385-7777
10 a.m. to 6 p.m. weekdays and Sun, open till 9 p.m. Fri and Sat

This small Victorian-themed chapel is located in the back of San Francisco Sally's Bridal and Formal Wear Rentals. It's a bit small, very pink, and could use some dusting, but maybe all of that adds to the Victorian flavor. Couples can dress as southern belles and beaux, in Western attire, or in traditional wedding garb, which can be rented in the front in the shop. It's tiny and a bit strange, but for one-stop shopping it is convenient. Packages start at $100.

A Special Memory Wedding Chapel
800 South Fourth St.
(702) 384-2211
www.aspecialmemory.com
8 a.m. to 10 p.m. Sun through Thurs, open till midnight Fri and Sat

Fashioned after a New England church and located a block away from Las Vegas Boulevard and very close to the license bureau, this quaint chapel is a nice retreat from the urban jungle that is downtown. Here you can choose from small and large chapels or the Lover's Lane drive-up window. For those Elvis lovers, the Elvis package includes the King driving you to and from the chapel in . . . yep, a 1955 pink Cadillac. Packages start at $199.

Vegas Weddings
555 South 3rd St.
(702) 933-3464
www.702wedding.com
Daily 8 a.m. to midnight

This new 9,000-square-foot building houses three wedding chapels and has the traditional look of a church with a gabled roof and Chablis stones framing the high arched authentic stained glass windows. The largest chapel is the spitting image of a traditional church, complete with automatic entry double doors and crystal chandeliers. For those really in a hurry, this chapel has the only walk-up wedding window in the world. Prices range from $40 to $2,800.

An adjoining large reception hall, a rare find in Las Vegas, can be used for after-ceremony celebrations. Go to their Web site to browse wedding specials, which include free upgrades and discounts during certain hours.

Viva Las Vegas Wedding Chapel
1205 Las Vegas Blvd. South
(702) 384-0771
www.vivalasvegasweddings.com
Daily 10:30 a.m. to 10 p.m.

Choices here are endless if you are looking for a theme wedding—Elvis complete with a pink Cadillac entrance for the bride (the car actually drives into the chapel), Blue Hawaii Elvis, young Elvis, Phantom, Liberace, Star Trek, etc. The larger chapel houses up to 100 guests and the themed '50s diner seats 35. Packages start at $199. After taking their vows, couples can see their names in lights on the neon sign located in the front. Viva Las Vegas has a nondiscrimination policy and same-sex couples are welcome.

ALL IN THE FAMILY: FREE AND CHEAP STUFF FOR KIDS

*"Each day of our lives we make deposits in
the memory banks of our children."*

—CHARLES R. SWINDOLL

It's been about a decade since some Las Vegas resorts tried to market themselves as family destinations. The emphasis on fun for the kiddies has since given way to marketing dance clubs and $300 bottles of Kristal to 20-somethings. But is Sin City—a town started by a gangster and built on blackjack, booze, and babes—any place to bring the kids? You bet it is. Las Vegas is definitely a playground for adults, but if you have the kids in tow there are plenty of fun attractions and things to do and see for the entire family.

ACTIVITIES **FOR** KIDS

Bonnie Springs Ranch
1 Gunfighter Lane
(702) 875-4191
www.bonniesprings.com
$20 per car

This cheesy Wild West theme park offers horseback riding; an old town including a blacksmith shop, working mill, saloon, and general store; a museum; a silver mine; and a petting zoo. Throughout the day there are also staged shows including bank robberies and shootouts.

Cranberry World West
1301 American Pacific Dr.
(702) 566-7160
Free

A brief film on growing and harvesting cranberries sets the stage for the free tour, which takes visitors through a small museum and along an assembly line to watch bottles of cranberry-blend drinks being bottled at a rate of 600 per minute. The tour ends at a bank of fountains a la Willie Wonka where visitors can drink their fill of every kind of cranberry drink the Ocean Spray company produces.

Dynamic Motion Simulators at Excalibur

3870 Las Vegas Blvd. South
(877) 750-5464
www.excalibur.com
$7

Several of the city's casinos have climbed aboard the trend of showing flicks in IMAX and 3-D. Among them, Excalibur Hotel has the Dynamic Motion Simulators, where guests watch a high-definition film while sitting in seats that move in sync to the on-screen action, including three different movie experiences.

Ethel M Factory Tour

Ethel M
1 Sunset Way
(702) 458-8864
www.ethelschocolates.com
Free

You can take a brief walk through the large cactus garden before heading into the glassed-in factory assembly line where chocolates are cooked, shaped, decorated, and packaged. There is also a cool M&M gift shop at the beginning of the self-guided tour, but the most popular spot is the candy store at the end where each visitor gets to choose a free sample.

Fountains at Bellagio

3600 Las Vegas Blvd. South
(702) 693-7111
www.bellagio.com
Free

Kids will love the more than 1,000 dancing fountains soaring as high as 240 feet above Lake Bellagio. At night the sophisticated music and light show adds to this magical free spectacle. Shows are every half hour starting early afternoon, every 15 minutes from 7 p.m. to midnight.

Fremont Street Glitter Gulch

Fremont Street, between Main Street and Las Vegas Boulevard
(702) 678-5777
Free

This arched-style canopy resembles a giant video game on steroids, with colorful lights and chest-pumping music. The Viva Vision screen mesmerizes onlookers with more than 12,000 synchronized LED lights. Hourly from 8 p.m. to midnight.

Gameworks
3785 Las Vegas Blvd. South
(702) 432-4253
www.gameworks.com
Free entrance

With more than 200 games and interactive attractions, this arcade is a good place for kids to spend their energy. It features a little bit of everything, including shooting games such as Virtual Cop, sports games, driving games, and anything else you can imagine.

Players can play Dance Dance Revolution, drive Indy 500 cars, surf, ride Jet Skis, shoot bad guys, or hang glide, all for the same price. The retro game area, which is sure to make parents feel old, includes old faves such as Missile Command, Galaga, Centipede, and Ms. PacMan. These throwbacks still cost a quarter a game, just like they did in 1981.

No game costs more than 99 cents. Park in the Showcase Mall garage and ask the attendant for a sheet of coupons, including a slip good for $10 worth of games at Gameworks.

Hoover Dam
Highway 97
(702) 494-2517
www.usbr.gov/lc/hooverdam.com
$30

Built during the Depression to harness the power of the often-destructive Colorado River and provide electrical power to Las Vegas and Southern California, this massive structure—considered one of the engineering marvels of the world—stands 726 feet tall and measures 660 feet thick. Take a self-guided tour, visit the art gallery, and view a film about the making of the dam.

To reach Hoover Dam, take I-15 south to I-215 east. Travel east on I-215 for approximately 10 miles to the junction of I-215 and US 93/US 95. Exit right headed south on US 93/US 95. Take US 93/US 95 south to Boulder City. Five miles from Boulder City, US 93/US 95 will split. Continue south on US 93 into Boulder City. Follow the signs to the Hoover Dam.

IMAX RideFilm at Circus Circus
2880 Las Vegas Blvd. South
(702) 734-0410
www.circuscircus.com
$7

Circus Circus's latest IMAX RideFilm, *ReBoot—The Ride*, a four-minute, twenty-second experience, is a sort of roller coaster ride through a giant city that exists inside a computer. It is shown on a 14-foot, 180-degree wraparound screen, with high-definition projection and digital sound.

Imperial Palace Auto Collection
Imperial Palace Hotel
3535 Las Vegas Blvd.
(702) 731-3311
www.autocollections.com
$8.95 or free with coupon on Web site

Placards tell the history of more than 200 cars and many are shown with mannequins in period clothing. A large anteroom contains a whole herd of Rolls Royces and—it is Vegas after all—an ornate bar you might have expected to find in a posh men's club of the 1880s. Among the autos on display are wheels used by John Wayne, Elvis Presley, Steve McQueen, and Liberace.

Las Vegas Mini-Grand Prix
1401 North Rainbow Rd.
(702) 259-7000
www.lvmgp.com
$3.25 kiddie karts, $6.50 go cart road course

Visitors put their driving skills to the test in Kiddie Karts (for those four years old and up), Go-Karts (54 inches and taller), Grand Prix Cars, and Super Stock Cars. After ripping up the raceway, check out the arcade.

Lied Discovery Children's Museum
833 Las Vegas Blvd. North
(702) 382-3445
www.ldcm.org
$8 adults, $7 kids

This downtown hands-on learning museum housed in a library is fun and educational for the entire family. Change a car tire, fix some plumbing, learn about saving and spending in the fake grocery store, enjoy making huge bubbles, or experience hurricane strength winds in the wind tunnel.

M&M World
3785 Las Vegas Blvd. South
(702) 736-7611
www.mymms.com
Free

Kids will love this emporium dedicated to these tiny chocolate coated candies, including a cute 3-D movie and four floors of chocolate heaven. Browse through hundreds of keychains, mugs, charms, and other tchotchkes, then move up to the second floor to view the rainbow wall of M&Ms in every color. The upper floors have more M&M merchandise, including games, home decor, and clothes.

MGM Grand Lion Habitat
3799 Las Vegas Blvd. South
(702) 891-7777
www.mgmgrand.com
Free

The MGM Grand Lion Habitat provides visitors not only a learning opportunity but a chance to see descendants of the original MGM lion, Leo. The multilevel habitat is in the middle of the resort where families can watch the kings of the jungle lounge, play, and eat daily. Placards around the habitat provide educational tidbits about the lions.

Shark Reef
Mandalay Bay
3950 Las Vegas Blvd. South
(702) 632-4555
www.mandalaybay.com
$17 adults, $12 children

If the Mandalay Bay can install a beach in the desert, what's to prevent them from bringing in the fish? Nothing. At the Shark Reef, you can walk through a tunnel filled with 1 million gallons of salt water where sharks, giant turtles, eels, and other fish are swimming above and around you. If you are staying at the Mandalay Bay, ask for free or discounted coupons for this exhibit at check-in.

Siegfried and Roy's Secret Garden and Dolphin Habitat
Mirage
3400 Las Vegas Blvd. South
(702) 791-7111
www.mirage.com
$15 adults, $10 children

This educational and entertaining experience at the Mirage includes a guided tour through the dolphin habitat and a walk through the small but fascinating open-air zoo. The zoo is filled with rare and breathtaking royal white lions, leopards, and an elephant, which the retired magicians have kept from extinction. The dolphin tank houses the mammals in a 2.5 million gallon tank where families can watch them frolic.

Springs Preserve
333 South Valley View Blvd.
(702) 822-7700
www.springspreserve.org
$18 adults, $10.95 children

Only 10 minutes away from the smoke and vice of the Strip, this educational complex covers 180 acres and houses exhibits, gardens, native trails, an arcade, and interactive displays including a cool flash flood re-creation. The insect and reptile display is also worth a visit.

AMUSEMENT **RIDES**

Buffalo Bill's Hotel and Casino
31900 South Las Vegas Blvd.
(702) 679-7433
www.primmvalleyresorts.com
Desperado, $8
Turbo Drop, $6

Area 51

When you tire of the flashing lights on Las Vegas Boulevard, it's time to get out of town. Way out. And search for flashing lights of another kind.

Head for Area 51—the crosshairs between wide-eyed alien enthusiasts and the stone-faced military boys. This popular location among UFO aficionados, and its famous military facility, are the inspiration for *The X-Files*.

Area 51 is inside the sprawling Nellis Air Force Base north of Las Vegas, squeezed in next to the Nevada Test Site. The U-2 spy plane flew there in the '50s; and more recently, the SR-71 Blackbird, the F-117A stealth fighter, and the B-2 stealth bomber. Presumably, lots of other high-tech research goes on there, but we're not authorized to know.

With all the science comes a strong dose of science fiction. Because it's so secret and secure, the stories go, Area 51 is where the government took the aliens and their spacecraft that crash-landed in Roswell, New Mexico, in the 1940s. Some folks claim they saw the charred bodies. Some say they worked on otherworldly spacecraft at Area 51. Reports of strange hovering lights and eerie shapes in the sky are routine.

To get there, head north on I-15 to US 93, a two-lane road that arrows through empty desert for 100 miles. Then turn left on the E.T. Highway (yes, that is actually the name of the highway). The highway is a two-lane stretch of road between Alamo and Tonopah, and rivals its counterpart to the north, US Hwy 50, for the title of "loneliest road." Chances are you won't see many other vehicles, let

Ride outside and through the casino on Desperado, a steel hypercoaster located at Buffalo Bill's just off I-15. Riders experience a series of drops and speeds up to 75 mph during the 1-mile long ride. Whisk up a 180-foot tower in under a minute during the Turbo Drop ride. After taking in the view from the top, riders are plunged to the bottom at 45 mph.

alone unidentified flying objects, on your drive through the desert. The only settlement on this isolated highway is Rachel—a scattering of mobile homes that house the town's 98 residents.

Rachel gained worldwide attention in April 1996 when the 98-mile state Route 375 was officially designated the Extraterrestrial Highway. More than 200 reporters, politicians, celebrities, and onlookers converged on the town for the dedication.

Yet even before Route 375 received its official moniker, Rachel was a gathering place for UFO buffs. Its proximity to Area 51 meant that there were numerous reports of strange lights and odd-shaped crafts.

Rachel is home to the A'Le'Inn, a lunch spot (where you can get an ABC, or Alien Burger with Cheese), site of numerous scenes in sci-fi movies including *Independence Day*, hotel, and anything-to-do-with-an-alien gift shop.

You can also visit the famous "Black Mailbox", which is now a white bulletproof mailbox. Located at the intersections between Highway 375 and Mailbox Road, it was originally installed by Steve and Glenda Medlin when postal delivery began in the area in the mid 1970s. It is located 6 miles from their cattle ranch. They had to replace the original black box due to looting by alien-loving tourists.

Some people opened the couple's mail, hoping to intercept classified correspondence. Some camped at the mailbox and a few crazies shot at it, leaving holes in the Medlins' bills and junk mail. Soon after, the couple attached a second box solely for the alien-seekers. It has a mail slot and is labeled ALIEN on one side and DROP BOX on another.

New York New York
3790 Las Vegas Blvd. South
(866) 815-4365
www.nynyhotelcasino.com
$14 per ride

Let the good times roll at the Manhattan Express roller coaster, where you can ride through a replica of the Big Apple featuring corkscrews, loops and a 540-degree spiral.

Sahara *closed 5/16/11*

2535 Las Vegas Blvd. South
(707) 737-2654
www.nascarcafelasvegas.com
Speed—The Ride, $10

If you feel the need for speed head to the Sahara to board Speed—The Ride. Climb into the supercoaster inside the NASCAR Café and ride through the Sahara's 192-foot-tall marquee and several loops before being propelled through the whole thing again—in reverse.

Stratosphere

2000 Las Vegas Blvd. South
(702) 380-7707
www.stratospherehotel.com
X-Scream, Insanity, and The Big Shot
$27.95 for all three rides

The Stratosphere is the place for the ultimate thrill rides. What's scarier than being 1,000 feet above ground? How about being 1,000 feet above ground and dangling off a building on a ride that only uses a lap bar to hold you in? Resembling a roller coaster cart, the X-Scream ride goes as fast as 30 mph and dangles riders more than 30 feet off the top of the hotel. Yikes.

Insanity is a huge mechanical claw extending over 60 feet off the edge of the Stratosphere Tower at a height of 900 feet. It spins riders at speeds up to three Gs. If you're brave enough to open your eyes you get a great view of downtown. Just try not to throw up on the people below.

The Big Shot is a free fall ride that shoots up 160 feet to the top of the Stratosphere Tower, making it the highest thrill ride in the world at 1,081 feet. After a few seconds at the top riders drop at a rate of 45 mph.

PLAYGROUNDS

Aliante Nature Discovery Park
2600 Nature Park Dr.

This fenced-in park is filled with a nice water fountain, playground, and Dino Dog sandbox housing replicas of fossilized dinosaurs including a giant skull on which children can play. There's also a smaller playground for little kids, a big kid slide area, and a man-made lake perfect for strolling around or feeding the ducks.

Paradise Park
4775 McLeod Dr.

Here there are plenty of free grills for family barbeques, as well as a large playground with plenty of equipment, basketball courts, a rec center, pool, and exercise route. Families can reserve the several covered areas with the parks and rec department for larger parties.

Pump It Up
7685 Commercial Way

3200 West Sunset Rd.
(702) 568-5204

Do your kids have energy to bounce off the walls? Then Pump It Up is the place to come. In this huge indoor inflatable bounce house, for a mere $7 per kid they can jump, crawl, or slide to their heart's content. They also offer Pumpstart classes incorporating jumping, sing-alongs, and games at $10 per class.

Silverado Ranch Park
9855 Gilespie St.

This big 10,000-square-foot facility houses plenty of picnic tables, an amphitheater, a nice skate park, baseball and softball fields, and wide-open play areas.

AFTER **SCHOOL** PROGRAMS

Boys and Girls Clubs of Las Vegas
www.bgca.org

Lied Memorial Clubhouse
2850 South Lindell Rd.
(702) 368-0317

James Clubhouse
2530 East Carey Ave.
(702) 649-2656

Donald W. Reynolds Clubhouse
2980 Robindale Rd.
(702) 614-8550

Boulder City Clubhouse
651 Adams Blvd.
(702) 293-2579

Andre Agassi Clubhouse
800 North Martin Luther King Blvd.
(702) 638-1120

West Las Vegas Family Resource Center
2850 South Lindell Rd.
(702) 932-1880

John D. "Jackie" Gaughan Clubhouse
920 Cottage Grove Ave.
(702) 731-6658

B.C. McCabe Clubhouse
2801 East Stewart Ave.
Las Vegas, NV 89101
(702) 388-2828

The Boys and Girls Clubs of Las Vegas offer a wide variety of activities for kids from ages five to eight. Clubs provide mentorships, academic help, career development, arts and crafts, and computer classes as well as sports programs. Fees are based on family income and no child is turned away.

YMCA
Kindergarten to grade 4, members $35 per week, non-members $59 per week
Middle school, members $43 per week, non-members $61 per week

Bill & Lillie Heinrich YMCA
4141 Meadows Lane

City of Las Vegas Durango Hills Community Center, Operated by the YMCA
3521 North Durango Dr.

City of Las Vegas Centennial Hills Community Center, Operated by the YMCA
6601 North Buffalo Dr.
www.ymca.net

YMCA after-school programs provide kids' activities, which are broken down into age groups, that include swimming, gymnasium games, study time, art, music, field trips, and snacks. The YMCA also offers a child watch program for kids from three months to seven years old so parents can work out while staff watches the kiddies. Free for all YMCA members.

SHOPPING:
SIN CITY BARGAINS

*"A bargain is something you can't use
at a price you can't resist."*
—FRANKLIN P. JONES

Las Vegas shopping is like most things the city does well—it's bigger, better, and more fun. Stores in Sin City are not just stores; they're the backdrop for shoppertainment.

Where else can a shopper experience an indoor thunderstorm, complete with rainfall, and never get wet? Or watch Bacchus, Venus, and Apollo come to life in a fountain of sound, light, and laser beams while admiring an adorable pair of Manolo Blahniks? How about window-shopping for the perfect Louis Vuitton clutch while eating a gelato along a fake Venetian Grand Canal?

From vintage clothing and wigs to haute couture, Las Vegas is a shopping maven's haven. But be warned, it's easy to drop a bundle in Sin City without ever hitting the slot machines or baccarat tables. Unless you know where to go, shopping can be just another high-stakes game. Like hard-core gamblers who rarely take time to sleep, serious shoppers can spend their money from 10 a.m. to midnight, 365 days a year.

WINDOW-SHOP **TILL** YOU **DROP**

Retailing as an art has achieved its highest form in Vegas. Catwalk designers have set up shop inside many high-roller casino resorts as well as a few noteworthy freestanding malls. A good place to window-shop and get ideas of what to look for at the outlets, consignment shops, and thrift stores is at the malls. Malls also provide a nice assortment of free or almost free "only in Vegas" entertainment, as well as lots of great people-watching.

Boca Park
8800 West Charleston Blvd.

If your significant other is allergic to shopping, drop them off at one of three neighboring golf courses on your way to Boca Park in Summerlin. Lined with trees and shrubs, this outdoor mall is where the locals shop and eat. Full of cheaper-than-Strip chain restaurants, including Mimi's Café, Claimjumper, The Cheesecake Factory, and a Whole Foods Market to boot, the mall also houses more than 20 retail stores, including everyone's affordable department store, Target.

Boulevard Mall
3528 South Maryland Pkwy.
(702) 732-8949
www.boulevardmall.com

This modern ultra mall houses 140 retail shops including department stores Dillards, Macy's, Sears, and JC Penney. A good alternative to the more crowded and flashy Fashion Show Mall if you have limited time to get your shopping fix. Head to the IHOP or McDonald's (located inside) for a cheap mega-breakfast before breaking the bank at the mall. Sign up for their club card and receive monthly e-mails with preferred offers, coupons, and info on upcoming sales.

Chinatown Plaza
4255 Spring Mountain Rd.
(702) 364-9600
www.lvchinatown.com

Yes, they really do have a Chinatown in Las Vegas. Complete with a gaudy gold statue of a Buddhist monk, you can find a 99 Ranch Market (full of great cheap Asian food), a jade gallery, Chung Chou City offering herbal cures for hangovers and other Sin City ailments, and a plethora of restaurants and shops in this two-story strip mall. The name is one of Vegas's many illusions, as a variety of Asian businesses—Filipino, Korean, Thai, and Vietnamese—are housed in the Pan-Asian complex.

Fashion Show Mall
3200 Las Vegas Blvd. South
(702) 784-7000
www.thefashionshow.com

With 2 million square feet, seven anchor department stores, and 250 other restaurants and boutiques, the Fashion Show Mall is one of the largest in the country. Shoppertainment here is the free flashy fashion shows on the 80-foot glass and metal runway offered every Friday, Saturday, and Sunday. The huge steel object hovering 130 feet above the mall entrance is "the cloud," a spaceship-like structure providing shade and a place to park it for weary shopaholics as well as music, flashing lights, and advertising screens broadcasting videos of Vegas attractions. Stop by the Visitor's Services booth (first floor at Macy's, near the cosmetics section) for your 11 percent off Welcome Savings Pass, valid for seven days.

The Fashion Show Mall also houses one of the many **Tix4Tonight** discount ticket booths. You'll find it directly under Neiman Marcus. Available shows and prices are listed at 9:30 a.m. daily and the box office opens at 10 a.m.

Showcase Mall
3785 South Las Vegas Blvd.
(702) 597-3122

This mall meets entertainment center houses M&M World, the Everything Coca-Cola Store, the Grand Canyon Experience, Ethel M Chocolates, and UA Cinemas. The gigantic M&M World delights chocoholics of all ages, with a 40-foot-long yellow bag of the miniature goodies beckoning visitors in that Vegas-neon sort of way. It offers more than 3,000 M&M logo items, from T-shirts to designer gowns (this is Vegas after all). Be sure to view the free *I Lost My M in Las Vegas* 3-D Movie. At Ethel M's flagship store, you can create your own custom assortment from 70 different varieties of gourmet chocolate (and get loads of free samples!). If you still need a sugar fix, head to the Everything Coca-Cola Store, possibly one of the only "real things" left in Sin City. Inhale **endless cups of free Coke** (the legal stuff) and sample products. Video junkies will love Gameworks, offering an assortment of virtual realty and sensory games.

Town Square Mall
6605 Las Vegas Blvd. South
(702) 269-5001
www.townsquarelasvegas.com

Located minutes from the airport, diehard shopaholics can make this outdoor mall their first stop in Sin City. Meander through more than 150 shops, dozens of restaurants, and a huge 9,000-square-foot park. Designed to resemble small-town USA, stores are housed in buildings with a variety of architectural motifs. Additionally, here you can shop below a real sky instead of the many fake ones at other Vegas themed malls on the Strip. Serious shoppers who want to rid distractions can send hubbies and little ones to the children's playground, tree house, maze, or 18-screen movie theater.

CASINO & RESORT **MALLS**

And they say gambling is addictive. Malls are also found in casinos throughout the Strip. Although they don't usually offer bargains they do provide lots of free entertainment and good window-shopping.

 The Forum Shops at Caesars Palace
3570 Las Vegas Blvd. South
(866) 227-5938
www.caesars.com

The Forum Shops are pure Vegas, baby, with plenty of luxury, glitz, and bling. More than 160 stores, restaurants, and specialty boutiques can be found in this Roman-themed retail therapy complex. Shops along pseudo-Roman streets run the gamut from Banana Republic to Gianni Versace. Some of the most expensive boutiques in the world are here, but discount shoppers can also delight in the variety of free entertainment and unique boutiques. Under color morphing Mediterranean skies, visitors can watch Baccus, Venus, and Apollo rotate, move, and speak at the Festival Fountain; view God of Thunder Atlas battle a wicked flying beast at the Fountain Show; and check out the 500 tropical fish in the 50,000-gallon saltwater aquarium. Standout stores include the fabulously huge FAO Schwartz toy store, Exotic Cars display of 50 cars and motorcycles, and the 13,000-square-foot Tourneau time dome, the largest watch store in the country.

Grand Canal Shoppes at the Venetian
3377 Las Vegas Blvd. South
(702) 414-4500
www.thegrandcanalshoppes.com

The cobblestone walkways at the Grand Canal Shoppes echo the real Venice, right down to the gondolas on the reproduction Grand Canal and St. Mark's Square. The Italian themed promenade is home to over 80 designer boutiques and restaurants as well as plenty of free entertainment. Stand on any of the bridges to overhear serenading gondoliers, or hover in St. Mark's square to watch a variety of singers, actors, magicians, jugglers, and stilt walkers.

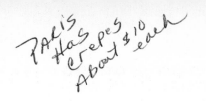
Paris Has crepes About $10 each

✓ Le Boulevard at Paris
3655 Las Vegas Blvd.
(877) 603-4386
www.parislasvegas.com

Always dreamed of seeing the City of Lights but can't afford a flight to gay Paree? Le Boulevard, a mini-me of Paris including French-inspired boutiques, a cobblestone replica of Rue de la Paix promenade, cafes, and bistros, can be found smack dab in the middle of the Strip. Stores replicate Paris prices as well as exteriors, but spendthrifts can **enjoy an inexpensive sweet or savory crepe** at Le Creperie under the cartoon-like blue sky amidst strolling gendarmes while people-watching for free.

Miracle Mile Shops at Planet Hollywood
3663 Las Vegas Blvd. South
(702) 785-5555
www.miraclemileshopslv.com

This streamlined high-tech mall offers an alternative for shoppers who aren't ridiculously rich. Over 170 generic shops including affordable Urban Outfitters, H&M, Gap, and American Apparel can be found in this urbanized contemporary mall. In addition to affordable prices, the deal here is the free acts and shows at the large stage outside of the V Theater. Magicians, Fab Four impersonators, comedians, and aerialists provide entertainment at no cost. The mall also features **a free fountain show** with lighted water effects, **a free laser show,** and a **free rainstorm show** outside of the Merchant's Harbor Coffee House.

SHOPPING **OUTLETS**

If the economy has you window-shopping at Bloomies with a padlock on your purse, you might want to broaden your horizons. Las Vegas is home to some of the most impressive shopping outlets that boast a slew of brand names at a fraction of mall costs.

Fashion Outlets Las Vegas

32100 Las Vegas Blvd. South
(702) 874-1400
www.fashionoutletlasvegas.com

Beside the California state line lies the bevy of boutiques found at the Fashion Outlets. The 100 shops are a decent mix between high-end (Ralph Lauren, Versace, Coach) and everyday (Gap, Guess, Nike). Foodies will love the Williams and Sonoma, and the World of Feng Shui will realign any power-shopping stress. A daily shoppers' shuttle runs from MGM Grand and Miracle Mile to the Fashion Outlets round-trip for $15.

Las Vegas Outlet Center

7400 South Las Vegas Blvd.
(702) 896-5599
www.premiumoutlets.com

Price tags of Strip stand-alone boutiques such as Juicy Couture, Ed Hardy, Michael Kors, Cole Haan, and many more are slashed and reslashed at the Las Vegas Outlet Center housing 130 retail shops. Same goes for stores that are staples at most malls across the US, such as Gap, Guess, and Ann Taylor. Heavy-hitting fashion labels can be found at Designer Fashion Clearance, where Manolos, Rock, and Republic jeans and La Perla lingerie are affordable for all thanks to the store's clearance prices. Park the kiddies on the giant carousel and shop till you drop. Join their VIP Club for free online coupons and e-mail sale updates.

Las Vegas Premium Outlets

875 South Grand Central Pkwy.
(702) 474-7500
www.premiumoutlets.com

Located five minutes from the Strip, this outlet is convenient and cheap. Aside from its central location, the mall boasts an attractive open-air village-style layout and nice merchant mix of 120 stores. Fashionistas will find a mountain of merchandise at Banana Republic, DKNY, Fossil, Max Studio, Polo, and many others.

EVEN **CHEAPER**: THRIFT **AND** CONSIGNMENT **SHOPS**

What's the old saying about walking a mile in another man's shoes? Well, never mind. What if they're another woman's shoes, say some gorgeous barely worn Italian stilettos that only cost $15? Pick your euphemism— designer resale, new-to-you, pre-owned, or just say it loud and proud: used clothes. Either way, if your taste exceeds your income here are a few places to find some retail treasures.

The Attic
1018 South Main St.
(702) 388-4088
www.theatticlasvegas.com

The Catch To shop at The Attic you need to pay a $1 for a lifetime entrance pass.

Here you can find funky fashions for the impossibly hip and all those trying to be. This huge vintage emporium, the largest used clothing store in the world, carries hats, wigs, lounge-lizard furnishings, and movie props, mostly from the '80s.

Buffalo Exchange
4410 South Maryland Pkwy.
(702) 791-3960
www.buffaloexchange.com

Stock up on your Bebe and Banana Republic at this savvy secondhand chain. Top-notch designer duds are a real bargain with everything from the 1940s to 1980s in vintage wear.

Catholic Charities St. Vincent Thrift Stores
1767 North Rancho Dr.
(702) 646-2150
www.catholiccharities.link.lv.com

All merchandise, mainly furniture, clothing, and household goods, is donated and resold to the public at a fraction of the retail price. The more you buy, the more you help fund feel-good programs offered to the needy by St. Vincent's. Special sales include half off for seniors on Tuesdays, men on Wednesdays, women on Fridays, and everyone on Thursdays.

Deseret Industries
4655 East Flamingo Rd.
(702) 547-0320

Proceeds from this vast thrift store support the Latter Day Saints. More warehouse than store, everything under the desert sun can be found here including furniture, musical instruments, tools, clothes, shoes, and books.

Goodwill of Southern Nevada
6344 West Sahara Ave. and other locations
(702) 364-5140
www.sngoodwill.org

With eight thrift store locations and more than 5,000 donations a week in the Valley, Goodwill is a goldmine for goodies including clothing, housewares, and jewelry at low, low prices. Stores also sponsor weekly sales—every Saturday seniors receive 50 percent off and on Toddler Tuesdays baby shopaholics get a break in prices. Over one-third of the goods sold at Goodwill are new merchandise, so it's worth a visit even if you don't like wearing used clothes.

Opportunity Village
921 South Main St.
(702) 383-1082
www.opportunityvillage.org

One of the largest thrift stores in the desert, this dumping ground for furniture, antiques, clothes, used cell phones, tools, and just about everything else stretches over an entire block. Raised money goes towards programs for the disabled.

Ritzy Rags Designer Resale Boutique
2520 South Rainbow Blvd.
(702) 257-2283

A tourist attraction in its own right, this store specializes in designer bargains.

You can complete your new outfit with some serious bling—their inventory also includes jewelry and fur collections.

Savers
3121 North Rancho Dr.
(702) 474-4773
www.savers.com

Savers buys used merchandise at a bulk rate from nonprofit organizations and slashes prices to sell to the public. A garage sale moved indoors, this well-laid-out gem offers almost-new clothes at dramatic discounts.

SPECIALTY **STORES** AND **BOUTIQUES**

Some things you can only find in Vegas, and many are sold in specialty stores and boutiques. Here are places where you can find unique knick-knacks, keepsakes, and souvenirs at a savings.

Bass Pro Shops Outdoor World
8200 Dean Martin Dr.
(702) 730-5200
www.basspro.com

Spread over two levels, this enormous 165,000-foot supply store specializes in fishing, hunting, and camping gear and apparel. It also includes a 40,000-gallon aquarium, indoor archery range, and a rock-climbing wall.

Bonanza Gift Shop
24640 Las Vegas Blvd. South
(702) 385-7359
www.worldslargestgiftshop.com

Here you can find a souvenir for just about anyone. The selection of gifts includes Sin City T-shirts, dice clocks, snow globes, posters, knickknacks, and an X-rated section. Stroll down aisle after aisle of everything from mugs and tote bags to moccasins and magnets, all at affordable prices.

Gambler's Book Shop

630 South 11th St.
(702) 382-7555
www.gamblersbook.com

It's a good bet that any book on gambling that you can name can be found at this store housing more than 1,000 books. Categories include sports betting, poker, casino games, the history of gambling, cheating detection, slots and video poker, biographies of mobsters, and Rat Pack-era entertainers.

Gambler's General Store

808 South Main St.
(702) 382-9903
www.gamblersgeneralstore.com

This 8,000-square-foot store feels like an old casino having a fire sale. Staff members, dressed like dealers and carrying gaming licenses, direct you to the dozens of choices of dice, miles of playing cards, and millions of poker chips. There are more than 35 types of chips in 19 colors with hundreds of designs. This is the only place in Vegas where it's easy to walk out with more chips in your pocket than you walked in with. You can also have chips custom made with your initials, company logo, or a picture of the kids.

Leonard's Wide Shoes

4480 Paradise Rd.
(702) 895-9993
www.leonardswideshoes.com

This specialty shoe shop carries every style and brand imaginable for hard-to-find wide and extra wide feet. Get lost in the 42,000 feet of inventory including sneakers, sandals, and dress shoes.

Michael's Used Bookshop

3430 East Tropicana Rd., Suite 9
(702) 434-1699
www.myspace.com/michaelsusedbooks.com

Bookworms will be drawn to the vast variety of literature at the local independent store. Their selection includes fiction, romance novels, true crime, mysteries, biographies, classic literature, and non-fiction titles.

Serge's Showgirl Wigs
953 East Sahara Ave.
(702) 732-1015
www.showgirlwigs.com

Join showgirls and drag queens at this superstore of wigs and hairpieces. The largest wig showroom in the country houses more than 10,000 wigs, full service stylists to help you with your new "do," and a celebrity wall of fame.

Z Castle
3375 Glen Ave.
(702) 641-3738
www.zcastle.com

Catering to those with a medieval bent, this store specializes in Renaissance garb, swords, and knives. The 1,000-foot store is crammed with costumes, jewelry, shields, and boots.

Zia Records
4225 South Eastern Ave.
(702) 735-4942
www.ziarecords.com

Some sounds get better the second or third time around. This indie music store houses a large new and used music and video selection. You can buy dozens of discs at just a few bucks as well as hear local live music performed on the little stage in the back. Sign up for a ZIA card to earn points that can go towards future purchases.

SWAP MEETS

Swap meets, aka the poor man's shopping mall, continue to thrive despite the poor economy. Vegas doesn't disappoint the die-hard haggler, with a nice assortment offering large crowds and plenty of deals.

Broadacres Swap Meet
2930 Las Vegas Blvd. North
(702) 642-3777

The Catch $1 admission fee.

Barter for used and new bargains at the valley's oldest and only outdoor swap meet, including diapers, tools, socks, and just about any other item that can legally be sold. Indulge in a delicious cheap lunch at one of the many food vendors offering exotic affordable arrays of Latin-style cooking.

Fantastic Indoor Swap Meet
1717 South Decatur Blvd.
(702) 877-0087

The Catch $1 admission fee.

This indoor swap meet lives up to its name with more than 600 shops chock full of merchandise—including clothes, shoes, jewelry, fragrances, silk flowers, and customized license plate frames. The large free parking, air-conditioning, on-site food court, free live entertainment, and only new merchandise for sale are all bonuses.

Rancho Swap Meet
2909 West Washington Ave.
(702) 631-1717
www.ranchoswapmeet.com

This free indoor swap meet is smaller than the others offering only new merchandise and bargains from about 50 stalls including cell phones, massage chairs, toys, videos, knives, baby clothes, and jewelry.

PAWN SHOPS

Las Vegas is the Mecca of pawn shops. These Smithsonians of missed dreams and second chances are pit stops for gamblers who have run out of cash but refuse to accept defeat. Their losses are shopaholics' gains at the dozens of pawn shops found in the desert. If you are tired of the homogenized offerings at national retailers, pawn shops are a good alternative to find a one-of-a-kind used gem. An entire list of pawn shops can be found in the appendix on page 190.

EZ Pawn Plus
1237 East Sahara Ave. and various other locations
(702) 693-6200

Another giant in the desert, EZ Pawn sells tons of tools as well as coins, guns, musical instruments, sporting goods, electronics, and jewelry.

Gold and Silver Pawn Shops
713 Las Vegas Blvd. South
(702) 385-7912
www.gspawn.com

The Catch If you want to go unnoticed hawking grandma's gold bracelet to finance your trip home after losing all your cash at the craps table, beware of cameras as the Gold and Silver Pawn Shop is the focus of the History Channel's reality show *Pawn Stars*.

This family-based business is a boutique-museum hodgepodge of items people have pawned. Rolexes, motorcycles, century-old rifles, Super Bowl rings, showgirl headdresses, and Olympic medals can all be found in this *Antiques Roadshow* with cash.

SuperPawn
1611 Las Vegas Blvd. South and various other locations
(702) 642-1133
www.cashamerica.com/superpawn.aspx

These Las Vegas pawn shops belong to a 40-plus empire in four states including Arizona, California, Nevada, and Washington. Jewelry is the big draw here, but stores also carry tools, electronics, sporting goods, guns, and a host of pre-owned merchandise.

FITNESS, FUN, AND GAMES:
CHEAP THRILLS

"Use it or lose it."

—JIMMY CONNORS

Las Vegas is not known for its athletic opportunities—the classic Vegas workout used to consist of lip-synching "Danke Shoen" along with Wayne Newton, hyperventilating a "hard eight" at the craps table, and swivel-hipping your way through a packed casino. But Sin City offers a wide variety of activities that are actually good for you, away from the smoke and alcohol-driven casinos. Whether it's biking, walking, working out, yoga, or other recreational activities, here are some inexpensive options that can make you feel better via the natural route.

MAJOR **PARKS**

Desert National Wildlife Refuge Complex
Corn Creek Road off US 95 North
(702) 879-6110
www.fws.gov/desertcomplex
Free

The Desert National Wildlife Refuge Complex houses four adjoining refuges that encompass millions of acres across the Mojave Desert. It is the largest refuge in the lower 48 states. Visitors can camp, hike, horseback ride, and backpack amidst plenty of critters, including the bighorn sheep that the complex protects.

Lake Mead National Recreation Area
601 Nevada Way
(702) 293-8990
www.nps.gov/lame
$5 per vehicle

One of the nation's most popular water-sun-and-sand destinations, the Lake Mead National Recreation Area offers camping, jet-skiing, kayaking, beautiful scenic drives, rafting, swimming, hiking, and fishing. More than 700 miles of shoreline offer a variety of activities to enjoy along the largest man-made body of water in the U.S.

Mount Charleston Park

Go north on US 95 and west on SR 156 or 157
(702) 515-5400
www.nv.gov
Free

Thirty-five miles northwest of Las Vegas in the Toiyabe National Park lies Mount Charleston, offering plenty of hiking and horseback riding in summer and sledding, tobogganing, and skiing in winter months. This high country destination commands magnificent views and is a great place to escape the scorching summer temperatures.

Red Rock Canyon State Park

SR 159, west of Las Vegas
(702) 363-1921
www.redrockcanyonlv.org
Free

Only a 20-minute drive from the Strip, this park's solitude and the red sandstone rock formations seem light-years away from the gaming tables. If you are really energetic, you can walk the 13-mile scenic route or drive to one of the many trailheads for short-distance hikes. It's also a favorite for mountain climbers and bikers. The Children's Discovery Trail is perfect if you plan on traveling with the tots. It covers less than a mile so everyone can make the journey.

Valley of Fire State Park

Go north on I-15 and take SR 169 at Crystal south to the park
www.parks.nv.gov
$6 per car

The Catch Temperatures get up to 120 degrees during summertime, so plan a visit in the fall, winter, or spring.

Located an hour from Las Vegas, Valley of Fire State Park is Nevada's oldest and largest park. It's aptly named and looks like a giant's sandbox in the high desert with 36,000 acres of bright red sandstone contrasting with the stark Mojave Desert. Visitors can hike, picnic, camp, mountain bike, and ride horses.

Zion National Park
US 9 near Springdale
(702) 435-772-3256
www.zionnational-park.com

The Catch Zion Park is a 2 ½-hour drive from Vegas, but definitely worth the haul.

This 229-square-mile national park offers outdoor splendor with towering cliffs, deep red canyons, and mesas as well as superb recreational opportunities. Visitors can camp, walk, backpack, swim, horseback ride, and hike in and around the winding Virgin River.

For a listing of all city parks see page 193 of the appendix.

RECREATION **CENTERS**

$1 a day, $5 per month, $25 per 6 months, $50 per year

A variety of recreation centers are sponsored through the City of Las Vegas Parks and Recreation Department. Most have fitness facilities with free weights and cardio machines, gymnasiums, pools, tennis, and golf courses. Many also offer six-week classes for as little as $15. Check the appendix section (on page 199) for a list of recreation centers.

CHEAP **YOGA**

Academy of Yoga
3012 Gilmary Ave.
(702) 735-3135
$9 per class

Here you can get your hatha yoga on from Sunday to Friday with a discounted rate of $85 for a series of 10 classes. Vinyasa, Kundalini, and power yoga classes are also offered.

All About Yoga
601 Whitney Ranch, Suite C-12
(702) 458-8088
www.yogainlasvegas.com

Part of the Stress Management Center of Nevada, this holistic center offers stress reduction programs as well as yoga classes for all levels. Classes range from $15 to $25, but they offer a beginner two for one special where you can get unlimited classes for eight weeks at half price if you sign up with a friend. Buy a six-week card and class prices go down to $12.50 per class. Their special Monday lunch time yoga classes are $64 for eight classes, bringing down prices to $8 per class.

Northwest Yoga Studio
7810 West Ann Rd. Suite 110
(702) 240-9996
www.northwestyogastudio.com

This yoga studio has something for everyone with classes tailored to seniors, mommies and kids, prenatal yoga, and basic to advanced instruction. Locals can take their first class for only $5! Buy a 10-class pass for $100 and bring down the cost to $10 per class. Classes are normally $12.

Studio 222
8645 West Flamingo Rd. Suite 104
(702) 769-2991

The Catch There is a suggested donation, but the amount you give is up to you.

Every Sunday morning, Studio 222 offers a free hatha yoga class. For beginners, it's a great way to ease into the practice of becoming a pretzel. The Men's Naked Yoga classes (yep, naked men!) on Tuesday and Friday nights are also on a pay-what-you-can basis.

CHEAP **PLACES** TO **SWIM**

Baker Pool
1100 East St. Louis Ave.
(702) 229-1532
Daily fees: ages 0 to 3 free, 4 to 7 $1, 18 to 49 $2, age 50+ $1.50
Summer passes: Individual $40, Family $60

This 25-yard outdoor pool features six lanes, diving boards, shaded areas, pool toys, and swimming lessons.

Carlos L. Martinez and Darrio J. Hall Family Pool
889 North Pecos Rd., corner of Washington Avenue and Pecos Road
Daily fees: ages 0 to 3 free, 4 to 7 $1, 18 to 49 $2, age 50+ $1.50
Summer passes: Individual $40, Family $60

This outdoor pool includes six lanes, diving boards, a slide, water play features, and swimming and water exercise classes.

Doolittle Pool
1950 North J St.
(702) 229-6398
Daily fees: ages 0 to 3 free, 4 to 7 $1, 18 to 49 $2, age 50+ $1.50
Summer passes: Individual $40, Family $60

This outdoor pool features an adult and children's diving board, a slide, shaded seating areas, picnic tables, and lockers and offers swimming and water exercise classes.

Garside Pool
300 South Torrey Pines Dr.
(702) 229-6393
Daily fees: ages 0 to 3 free, 4 to 7 $1, 18 to 49 $2, age 50+ $1.50
Summer passes: Individual $40, Family $60

This 25-yard outdoor pool with six lanes features a diving board, pool toys, shaded areas, and picnic tables and offers swimming lessons.

Municipal Pool

431 East Bonanza Rd.
(702) 229-6309
Daily fees: ages 0 to 3 free, 4 to 7 $1, 18 to 49 $2, age 50+ $1.50
Summer passes: Individual $40, Family $60

This 50-meter, 25-yard indoor pool has three springboards, two outdoor pavilions, a fitness room, lockers, and pool toys and offers swimming and water exercise classes.

Pavilion Center Pool

101 South Pavilion Center Dr.
(702) 229-1488
Daily fees: ages 0 to 3 free, 4 to 7 $1, 18 to 49 $2, age 50+ $1.50
Summer passes: Individual $40, Family $60

This 25-yard outdoor pool has three diving boards, shaded seating areas, lockers, and pool toys and offers group and private swimming lessons.

CHEAP **GOLF**

Las Vegas is typically known for greed and gambling, not greens; blackjack and not bogeys. Today, in addition to the glitz and glamour, golf has become a lure for many Vegas visitors. There's more to golf courses than softly rolling green hills and neatly combed sand traps. Desert courses offer stunning sunrise and sunset golf skies with vibrant brown, red, and purple colors; gorgeous backdrops of rugged mountain ranges; putting amidst cacti; and affordable spring and summer rates. Check the appendix on p. 201 for a complete listing of public courses.

Badlands Golf Club

9119 Alta Dr.
(702) 242-4653
Desperado Course: 9 holes over 3,137 yards with a par of 36
Diablo Course: 9 holes over 3,293 yards with a par of 36
Outlaw Course: 9 holes over 3,038 yards
Fees start at $80

Three 9-hole courses combine to make this Johnny Miller designed track one of the top desert golf experiences. Set amid the Red Rock Mountains, they are worth the twenty-minute drive from the strip.

Black Mountain Golf & Country Club

500 Greenway Rd.
(702) 565-7933
Desert 9 Course: 9 holes over 3,295 yards with a par of 36
Founders Course: 9 holes over 3,309 yards with a par of 37
Horizon 9 Course: 9 holes over 3,241 yards with a par of 36
Fees start at $75

Black Mountain offers three options, the Desert, Founders, and Horizon nine-hole courses to get your golf on. Each has plush Bermuda grass and dozens of mature Cypress, pine, ash, and olive trees providing generous shade in summer months.

Las Vegas Paiute Golf Resort

10325 Nu Wav Kaiv Blvd.
(800) 711-2833
Sun Mountain Course: 18 holes over 7,112 yards with a par of 72
Snow Mountain Course: 18 holes over 7,146 yards with a par of 72
Wolf Course: 18 holes over 7,604 yards with a par of 72
Fees start at $100

Designed by Pete Dye, these courses provide challenges for any golfer at reasonable fees. The newest and most difficult Wolf is the longest in Nevada and meanders up and over rugged gold and red rock canyons, providing stunning views throughout the course.

Rio Secco Golf Club

2851 Grand Hills Dr.
(888) 867-3226
Rio Secco Course: 18 holes over 7,332 yards with a par of 72
Fees start at $90

One of the most challenging courses in Vegas, Rio Secco takes players into the canyons and on top of plateaus. Designed by Rees Jones, it features little water and lots of natural desert surroundings. It is home to the Butch Harmon School of Golf.

EDUCATION:
LOW-COST LEARNING

"Nothing that is worth knowing can be taught."

—OSCAR WILDE

For penny-pinching folks seeking new skills, enrichment, or just enjoyment there are education programs offering a variety of courses and programs to satisfy almost every need and want. Here are some low and no cost havens for any cheap bastard trying to improve their skills or expand their intellectual horizons.

COLLEGE **COURSES**

Community College of Southern Nevada
www.csn.edu

Boulder City Campus
700 Wyoming St.
(702) 651-4040

Henderson Campus
700 College Dr.
(702) 651-3000

Charleston Campus
6375 West Charleston Blvd.
(702) 651-5000

Sahara West Center Campus
2409 Las Verdes St.
(702) 651-4487

Cheyenne Campus
3200 East Cheyenne Ave.
(702) 651-4000

Summerlin Center Campus
333 Pavilion Center Dr.
(702) 651-4900

Green Valley Center Campus
1560 West Warm Springs Rd.
(702) 651-2650

Western Center Campus
4601 West Bonanza Rd.
(702) 651-4800

The largest college in Nevada, the Community College of Southern Nevada offers multiple locations and flexible classes daily and nightly. Here you can learn a brand new career with classes in dentistry, economics, physical therapy, pharmacy technician training, psychology, and others on the cheap, or just pick up a new hobby by attending music, dance, theater, pottery, and painting classes. Nevada residents over 62 can audit or register for credit in any course for free.

University of Nevada, Las Vegas
4505 Maryland Pkwy.
(702) 895-3394
www.unlv.edu

The Division of Educational Outreach at UNLV offers leisure and recreational activities and courses in just about everything. Go bird watching or wine tasting, train your pooch, or learn how to manage your money for mere pennies (okay, a bit more than a few cents but very affordable). Go online to view the variety of courses and one-day seminars.

OTHER **DEALS** ON **CLASSES**

ArtSmart
1400 North Rampart Blvd.
(702) 525-2789

Here the art curriculum is based on art history and is specifically designed for young children (ages 2 to 10). In each session, children discover art through learning the history of art; exploring various artistic techniques, methods, and mediums; and creating their own works of art. Classes run about $12 per hour.

Computer Classes at Local Libraries
Sahara West Library
9600 West Sahara Ave.
(702) 507-3630

Summerlin Library
1771 Inner Circle Dr.
(702) 507-3860

West Charleston Library
6301 West Charleston Blvd.
(702) 507-3940

Don't know how to "tweet" or connect with friends on Facebook? Get into the technological age with classes on e-mailing, Facebook, word processing, Excel, the Internet, and lots of other techno topics. These free classes run from 10 a.m. to noon.

Michaels Arts & Crafts Stores

3355 East Russell Rd.
(702) 458-8355

9881 South Eastern Ave.
(702) 407-5690

1252 South Decatur Blvd.
(702) 259-0034

Cruise down the aisles at Michaels Arts & Crafts Store and you can't help but be inspired by some of the projects that you can do at home with the kids or the materials you can use for classes, gifts, or parties. Every Saturday from 10 a.m. to noon, the store hosts low-cost drop-in craft activities for ages 5 to 12. Other classes are offered throughout the year.

The store stocks paints for glass, fabric, and canvas; cake and candy making supplies; artificial flowers; loads of seasonal decor and crafts kits; and frames for those new masterpieces.

Pottery West

5026 North Pioneer Way
(702) 685-7573
www.potterywest.com

Pottery West is a kilnyard and pottery school and one of the few places in Sin City where you can get really dirty while remaining fully clothed. They offer a range of classes for beginner, intermediate, and advanced potters. For a real bargain, opt for the $95 pass and attend as many classes as you want during a seven-week period.

Summerlin Dance Southwest

7835 South Rainbow Blvd., Suite 5
(702) 897-5095
www.summerlindance.com

Kids can get down, dance, enjoy music classes, and participate in theater and performing arts presentations at Summerlin Dance Southwest. Tumbling and singing classes are here, too, as are classes for really little ones (age two). The best part? The first class is free for new students.

LIBRARIES

Centennial Hills Library
6711 North Buffalo Dr.
(702) 507-6100
Hours: Mon to Thurs, 9 a.m. to 9 p.m.; Fri to Sun, 10 a.m. to 6 p.m.

This state-of-the-art library offers a collection of books, music, movies, and other resources for adults and children of all ages, as well as a computer lab for adults, a Homework Help Center and adjoining computer lab for kids, an art gallery, story room, and used bookstore/café. It also offers free wireless Internet access.

Clark County Library
1401 East Flamingo Rd.
(702) 507-3400
Hours: Mon to Thurs, 9 a.m. to 9 p.m.; Fri to Sun, 10 a.m. to 6 p.m.

The Clark County Library serves as a regional resource for southern Clark County. The library houses a study room, Jewel Box Theater, storytime room, theater, and galleries.

Enterprise Library
25 East Shelbourne Ave.
(702) 507-3760
Hours: Mon to Thurs, 9 a.m. to 9 p.m.; Fri to Sun, 10 a.m. to 6 p.m.

The Enterprise Library serves the southwestern metropolitan area of Las Vegas and offers free wireless Internet access. It houses a storytime room and gallery.

Las Vegas Library
833 Las Vegas Blvd. North
(702) 507-3500
Hours: Mon to Thurs, 9 a.m. to 9 p.m.; Fri to Sun, 10 a.m. to 6 p.m.

The Las Vegas Library is the Library District's administrative headquarters. It offers free wireless Internet access, and houses special collections on government documents and local history and gaming.

Meadows Library

251 West Boston Ave.
(702) 474-0023
Hours: Mon to Thurs, noon to 8 p.m.; Sat, 10 a.m. to 3 p.m.

The 813-square-foot Meadows Library is located inside the Stupak Community Center. It is an outreach branch that offers materials in English and Spanish including books, DVDs, music CDs, and popular materials, as well as GED, ESL, and citizenships study materials. It also includes a children's area and two bilingual staff members to serve the community.

Sahara West Library

9600 West Sahara Ave.
(702) 507-3630
Hours: Mon to Thurs, 9 a.m. to 9 p.m.; Fri to Sun, 10 a.m. to 6 p.m.

The Sahara West Library features a computer center with 12 public computer workstations, a multipurpose room, and a used bookstore. The library houses the International Language Collection, a collection of books, magazines, newspapers, and videos in 37 different languages. It also offers free wireless Internet access.

Spring Valley Library

4280 South Jones Blvd.
(702) 507-3820
Hours: Mon to Thurs, 9 a.m. to 9 p.m.; Fri to Sun, 10 a.m. to 6 p.m.

The Spring Valley Library serves the communities in southwestern Las Vegas and houses the Asian Culture Collection. It offers free wireless Internet access.

Summerlin Library

1771 Inner Circle Dr.
(702) 507-3860
Hours: Mon to Thurs, 9 a.m. to 9 p.m.; Fri to Sun, 10 a.m. to 6 p.m.

The Summerlin Library is located in Summerlin Hills Park and houses a story room, courtyard, and gallery and offers free wireless Internet access. The adjacent 284-seat performing arts center provides ballet, musicals, plays, and dance performances.

West Charleston Library
6301 West Charleston Blvd.
(702) 507-3940
Hours: Mon to Thurs, 9 a.m. to 9 p.m.; Fri to Sun, 10 a.m. to 6 p.m.

The West Charleston Library is a large public library that offers traditional services for both adults and children. It offers a story room, lecture hall, gallery, and free wireless Internet access and houses a Health Sciences special collection.

West Las Vegas Library
951 West Lake Mead Blvd.
(702) 507-3980
Hours: Mon to Thurs, 9 a.m. to 9 p.m.; Fri to Sun, 10 a.m. to 6 p.m.

This library features the African American Special Collection consisting of specialized materials by and about African Americans, and the Library District's first dedicated Homework Help Center. The 1,540-square-foot center adjacent to the Young People's Library offers core print and electronic materials for students K–8 with a 20-seat dedicated homework help computer lab. The branch also offers free wireless Internet access.

PLACES **WITH** FREE **WI-FI**

Most high-speed Internet in Las Vegas is acquired for a fee from the business centers at the major hotel casinos. Sure, you can access it, but most hotels will charge at least $12 per day for the service. Here are some cheaper (and free) options if you want to go online.

Apple Stores
Caesars Palace
Forum Shops
3500 Las Vegas Blvd. South
(866) 227-5928

Fashion Show Mall
3200 Las Vegas Blvd. South
(702) 650-9550

Town Square
6671 Las Vegas Blvd.
(702) 221-8826
www.apple.com

Mac lovers can check out the latest iPad, iPhone, or laptop while searching the Web for free.

Buffalo Wild Wings
www.buffalowildwings.com

7430 Las Vegas Blvd. South, Suite 120
(702) 614-0238

7345 South Durango Dr., Suite 118–121
(702) 260-4800

4280 Hualapi #108
(702) 251-3911

617 Mall Ring Circle
(702) 456-1237

10271 South Eastern Ave., Suite 121
(702) 492-1880

190 West Craig Rd.
(702) 642-0055

150 East Centennial Pkwy.,
Suite 101
(702) 649-3054

65 Horizon Ridge Pkwy.
(702) 564-5795

6640 North Durango Dr., Suite 110
(702) 395-2455

This New York-style Buffalo chicken wing fast food joint not only serves up boneless wings, legs, and tenders, it also offers free wireless access.

Coffee Bean & Tea Leaf
Various locations
www.coffeebean.com

This family-owned business specializing in bringing specialty coffees and teas into the United States from various plantations around the world also offers free Wi-Fi. Grab a cup of joe or a fancy caffeinated concoction and search the Web free of charge.

Krispy Kreme
www.krispykreme.com

301 Fremont St.
(702) 366-0150

2880 Las Vegas Blvd. South
(702) 733-9944

1331 West Craig Rd.
(702) 657-9575

3850 Las Vegas Blvd.
(702) 736-5235

7015 West Spring Mountain Rd.
(702) 222-1813

9791 South Eastern Ave.
(702) 617-9160

At this retail donut chain, you can get the original scrumptious doughy delight brushed with a sugar coating or choose from a variety of lip smacking treats and also get free Wi-Fi to go along with a melt-in-your-mouth masterpiece.

McCarran International Airport
5757 Wayne Newton Blvd.
(702) 261-5211
www.mccarran.com

You can even get free Wi-Fi at the airport. McCarran offers free wireless access across 90 percent of its public areas. Passengers with wireless-enabled laptops or PDAs can access the Internet from nearly any public area for free.

McDonald's
Various locations
www.mcdonalds.com

Here you can get a really cheap meal (with special burgers for a buck!), really tasty fries, pretty good cheap coffee, and free Wi-Fi.

Panera Bread
Various locations
www.panerabread.com

This bright bread-themed café and bakery traveling at the speed of Starbucks (over 20 locations in Las Vegas and still expanding) offers soups, salads, artisan sandwiches, and pastries as well as free Wi-Fi.

Starbucks
Various locations
www.starbucks.com

Sure, it's a huge chain and every outlet looks about the same—green-and-white color scheme, high-tech furniture, coffee bean display—and offers about the same top-notch coffee drinks with consistency. But they also offer really comfy seating and free Wi-Fi.

RECREATION **CENTERS**

There are hundreds of programs available through the city's many recreation centers. Want to learn to play the violin, dance the samba, cook a pot roast, post something on Youtube, or sew? It's all here at reduced rates. Some classes last a day, and some are weekly for a few months. Check the appendix on page 199 for a list of recreation centers.

MUSEUMS AND ART GALLERIES:
CHEAP CULTURE

"I can't change the fact that my paintings don't sell. But the time will come when people will recognize that they are worth more than the value of the paints used in the picture."
—VINCENT VAN GOGH

There's no Louvre in Las Vegas and no British Museum—though you can admire a full-size replica of Michelangelo's *David* in the shopping arcade of Caesars Palace.

That marble *David* aside, Nevada's number one gambling resort does not leap quickly to mind as a prime repository of the world's cultural treasures.

Five years ago the concept of art in Las Vegas probably ran no deeper than paintings on black velvet. You know the kind—a tiger, a matador, some dogs playing poker. Art was more likely the name of your taxi driver than a painting or sculpture.

Then came the reinvention of the Strip with lavish resorts, celebrity-chef restaurants, boutique retail, and cutting edge entertainment. So why not art? Forget the lounge acts and the scantily clad cocktail waitresses; there lies an oasis of culture among these desert dunes of kitsch. Las Vegas actually boasts a dozen or so museums, some cast in a conventional mold and others downright eccentric. If you're seeking a change of pace from the mad whirl of the casino tables, they can provide ample diversion and occasional enlightenment. Mix the Picassos, Matisses, and Renoirs with some honky-tonk museums offering sparkling Liberace costumes, replicas of King Tut's tomb, and Elvis's Cadillac limo, and you've got more to do in Sin City than sit around and lose at Keno. Sure, some charge an entrance fee, but it's a lot less than you'll spend at the tables or slots in half an hour.

FREE **AND** ALMOST-**FREE** MUSEUMS

Atomic Testing Museum
755 East Flamingo Rd.
(702) 794-5161
www.atomictestingmuseum.org
Mon to Sat 9 a.m. to 5 p.m., Sun 1 to 5 p.m.
$12 adults, $9 children

Once America was done blowing up its atom bombs in the desert, scientists wondered what they could do with the facility. Make it into a museum, of course. The Atomic Testing Museum takes visitors through the freaky history of nuclear experimentation in Nevada. With the white-lab-coated tour guides and an underground testing gallery, this museum is a bit creepy.

Bellagio Gallery of Fine Art
3600 Las Vegas Blvd. South
(702) 693-7111
www.bellagio.com
Daily, 10 a.m. to 6 p.m.
$15

This world-class gallery houses a $300 million art collection. Works from masters Van Gogh, Cezanne, and Monet are comfortably removed from the craziness of the casino inside a small gallery beyond the conservatory. You can also get an audio tour narrated by owner Steve Wynn. In a town famous for replicas of New York, Paris, and Venice, it's nice to have something real to look at.

Boulder City/Hoover Dam Museum
1305 Arizona St.
(702) 294-1988
www.bcmha.org
Daily, 10 a.m. to 4 p.m.
Free

This small museum located in the downtown section of Boulder City features exhibits, films, and models explaining how and why the Hoover Dam was built; gives a sense of the daily lives of the workers and their families; and illustrates what conditions were like in the United States during the Depression.

Carroll Shelby Museum
6755 Speedway Blvd.
(702) 942-7325
www.shelbyautos.com
Mon to Fri, 8 a.m. to 4 p.m.
Free

Adrenaline junkies can head to car designer and racer Carroll Shelby's facility near the Las Vegas International Speedway to view newer model Series 1 and classic Cobras, as well as mint condition classic cars. From CSX2000, the first Cobra, to the latest Ford Shelby GT500 "Super Snake" and the first Ford GT prototype, the museum celebrates the life and cars of Shelby, featuring interactive displays, exhibits, a museum gift shop, and library. Free daily tours are held at 10:30 a.m.

Clark County Heritage Museum
1830 South Boulder Hwy.
(702) 455-7955
Daily, 9 a.m. to 4:30 p.m.
$1.50 adults, $1 seniors and children

This very cheap cool museum on the outskirts of the city includes interactive displays including the history of gaming in Las Vegas and rotating art collections. Outside is Heritage Street, a small tree-lined street housing historical structures as well as a Nevada ghost town.

Goldwell Open Air Museum
Near Rhyolite
(775) 553-0000
www.goldwellmuseum.org
Daily, open 24 hours
Free

Located near the ghost town of Rhyolite on the outskirts of Death Valley, this weird and kind of creepy eight-acre outdoor sculpture park houses a boarded-up shack and seven unlabeled giant sculptures. You'll think you just stepped into a Stephen King movie. Also be sure to explore the neighboring little town that was with its adjoining graveyard.

Howard W. Cannon Aviation Museum
McCarran International Airport
5757 Wayne Newton Blvd.
(702) 455-7968
Daily, open 24 hours

The open-air museum shows the history of aviation in Southern Nevada, from the first flight in 1920 through the introduction of the jet. Focusing on the history of commercial and general aviation, it's a great time-killer while waiting for your flight.

Imperial Palace Auto Collection

3535 Las Vegas Blvd. South
(702) 794-3174
www.autocollections.com
Daily, 9:30 a.m. to 9:30 pm
$8.95 adults, $5 children

Like metal dreams, they line up fender-to-fender on the white carpet. Polished chrome glitters. Fins sweep back. Grills poke forward. The 300 antique and classic cars in the Imperial Palace Auto Collection sit silently but conjure up the sounds of purring motors, crackling exhausts, and screeching brakes. Some are for sale, so if you win big you might be driving back home in style.

Las Vegas Historic Museum

Tropicana
3801 Las Vegas Blvd. South
(702) 739-2222
www.troplv.com
Daily, 9 a.m. to 9 p.m.
$7

This museum located in the Tropicana focuses on the Las Vegas underworld of gaming, mobsters, entertainers, and the brothels of Sin City. Statues of Bugsy Siegel, Al Capone, Frank Sinatra, and Dean Martin are housed here as well as plenty of TV monitors playing videos of Ol' Blue Eyes. Cool retro collectable items including decanters, chips, signs, and glasses from now-defunct hotels are also on display.

Las Vegas Natural History Museum

900 Las Vegas Blvd. North
(702) 384-3466
www.lvnhm.org
Daily, 9 a.m. to 4 p.m.
$10 adults, $5 children; Visit the museum's Web site to print out a discount coupon good for a free adult admission.

Great for inquisitive kids and grown ups alike, the natural-history museum on the Strip breathes lots of life into the stuffy subject of fossils. The dinosaur stars of the show are animated, made-in-Japan models of a Tyrannosaurus Rex and his friends. The museum houses aquariums, a snake pit, and exhibits featuring Egyptian artifacts and the African landscape.

Liberace Museum

1775 East Tropicana Ave.
(702) 798-5595
www.liberace.org
Mon to Sat, 10 a.m. to 5 p.m., Sun 1 to 5 p.m.
$15 (not free, but fabulous)

At the Liberace Museum, lavish props and costumes once employed by the flamboyant entertainer tell a good part of the story of the most unique performer to ever grace a Las Vegas stage. The museum itself is separated into a trio of white brick buildings housing a library with hundreds of photos and personal papers, an extensive selection of miniature pianos, his prized collections of silver and crystal and, of course, an exhibit of the over-the-top sequins-and-fur capes he wore onstage to the delight of millions of bemused fans.

Lost City Museum of Archeology

721 South Moapa Valley Blvd.
(702) 397-2193
www.comnett.net
Thurs to Sun, 8:30 a.m. to 4:30 p.m.
$3

Located south of the city of Overton, this museum houses an extensive collection of early Pueblo Indian artifacts. Built on the ruin of a Virgin Anasazi pueblo, it includes a full scale reconstruction of an Indian pueblo structure as well as pottery and art exhibits.

Magic and Movie Hall of Fame

3555 Las Vegas Blvd. South
(702) 737-1343
Tues to Sat, 10 a.m. to 6 p.m.
$10; Includes free afternoon magic shows, featured in the
Houdini Theater.

This 20,000-square-foot attraction houses exhibits and memorabilia on ventriloquism, magic, and the movies. Get spooked by the famous ventriloquist dummies or act like Tom Hanks in *Big* and test your luck with the antique fortune teller machines.

Neon Museum

Fremont Street Galleries
(702) 229-6301
Daily, 24 hours
Free

The golden age of neon lives on at this boneyard for old huge lighted signs of yesteryear's Strip. Saved from the scrap heap and housed at the entrance of the Fremont Street Experience, these vintage signs can be viewed 24/7 for free.

Nevada Southern Railroad Museum

600 Yucca St.
(702) 486-5006
www.museums.nevadaculture.com
Sat and Sun, rides at 10 a.m., 11:30 a.m., 1 p.m., and 2:30 p.m.
$8 adults, $4 children

Thomas the Tank Engine lovers will appreciate this kiddie-friendly museum and train park, which was built in 1931 as a railroad off the Union Pacific tracks. You can take a 45-minute ride on a replica Pullman train, visit the gift shop, and stroll around the depot. Visit the Web site for $1-off coupons.

Nevada State Museum and Historical Society

700 Twin Lakes
(702) 486-5205
Daily, 9 a.m. to 5 p.m.
$4 adults, children under 17 free

Get a non-glitzy glimpse of Nevada's history through a variety of displays highlighting the 41st state. The dinosaur exhibit, desert wildlife display, and Native American history sections are worth a visit. Bring a picnic and lunch by the lake at the adjacent Lorenzi Park.

Pinball Hall of Fame

1610 East Tropicana Ave.
(702) 434-9746
www.pinballhall.org
Daily, 11 a.m. to 11 p.m.
Free

Test your flipper skills on hundreds of playable machines and arcade games dating from the 1950s to the present. Both a pinball museum and arcade, profits from the games (which cost just a quarter each) go to local charities.

ART **GALLERIES**

Art Encounter
3979 Spring Mountain Rd.
(702) 227-0220
www.artencounter.com
Hours: Tues to Friday 10 a.m. to 6 p.m.; Sat and Mon, noon to 5 p.m.
Free

The largest fine art gallery in Nevada is located just five minutes from the Strip and features originals by more than 100 local, national, and international artists in 8,000 square feet. In addition to viewing giclees, fine art, and paintings, you can also get art appraised and framed.

Bluestone Gallery
2240 Village Walk Dr., #132
(702) 458-9979
Hours: Mon to Wed, 10 a.m. to 8 p.m.; Thurs to Sat, 10 a.m. to 9 p.m.; Sun, 11 a.m. to 6 p.m.
Free

Specializing in local artists, this gallery is adjacent to the Green Valley Ranch Casino, so you can spend your winnings on selections from their large collection of impressionist paintings. Subjects include European destinations, Las Vegas, and jazz artists. They also have a huge collection of glass art.

Carrara Galleries
1236 Rainbow Blvd.
(702) 877-4299
Hours vary, call ahead.

This gallery offers a superb selection of fine art with works from masters including Dali, Peter Max, and Picasso, as well as mixed medium work, limited collection signed prints, bronze sculptures, and affordable prints from over 100 artists.

Collectors Fine Art
30 Via Brianza St., Suite 120
(702) 558-5078
Hours: Daily, 10 a.m. to 8 p.m.
Free

Contemporary, local, and 20th-century artists are featured at this modern gallery.

Contemporary Arts Collective
101 East Charleston Blvd.
(702) 382-3886
www.lasvegascac.org
Hours vary, call ahead.
Free

Sponsored by a nonprofit organization, this gallery combines showings of innovative contemporary artwork including visual, media, performing, and literary art to inspire Warhol wannabes.

Donna Beam Fine Art Gallery (UNLV)
4505 South Maryland Pkwy.
(702) 895-3893
www.donnabeamgallery.unlv.edu
Hours: Mon to Fri, 9 a.m. to 5 p.m.; Sat, 10 a.m. to 2 p.m.
Free

Part of the University of Nevada, Las Vegas, this gallery is open to college and non-student art aficionados. Exhibits represent all kinds of media including national and local artists.

Edward & Edward Fine Art
1039 South Main St., Suite 150
(702) 240-2787
Hours vary, call ahead.
Free

Named after artist Edward Sobanski, a famous Polish artist and master wood sculptor who is partially blind, this gallery houses more than 60 of his paintings, wood sculptures, and bronze castings. The gallery is the largest in the nation housing items by Sobanski.

Eternal Treasures
1725 South Rainbow Blvd., Suite 5
(702) 256-9134
Hours vary, call ahead.
Free

One of 13 franchises, this flagship gallery features religious as well as inspirational fine art. Here you can find original paintings of Jesus, Buddha, and other religious heavy hitters in oil, acrylics, water colors, and pastels.

G-C Arts
1217 South Main St.
(702) 452-2200
Hours vary, call ahead.
Free

On the first Friday of every month this contemporary downtown gallery sponsors visual and performing art as well as their daily painting exhibits. The gallery is open and airy, with displays featuring established contemporary artists such as Raymond Pettibon, Richard Serra, and James Turrell.

Glass Artistry, Inc.
4200 West Desert Inn Rd.
(702) 221-8494
Hours vary, call ahead.
Free

Butterfingers should stay away from this unique gallery featuring glass works of art. Everyone else should make a stop at the only all-glass gallery in Nevada, featuring sculptures, etched and carved mirrors, bowls, and plates.

Indian River Gallery
3663 Las Vegas Blvd. South, Suite 680
(702) 598-3929
www.indianrivergallery.com
Hours: Sun to Thurs, 10 a.m. to 11 p.m.; Fri and Sat, 10 a.m. to midnight
Free

Lovers of Southwest Navajo art don't have to travel away from the Strip to find sculptures, weavings, paintings, jewelry, pottery, antiques, hand woven baskets, and other pieces of art. All are housed in the Miracle Mile shops.

Michael Godard Art Gallery & Store
3700 West Flamingo Rd.
(702) 363-4278
www.michaelgodard.com
Hours vary, call ahead.
Free

This very Vegas gallery features work from rockstar artist Michael Godard. Dozens of his unusual paintings of olive people, martinis, and flaming dice can be found in framed prints, apparel, and gift items.

Moonstruck Gallery
6820 West Sahara Ave., Suite 9
(702) 364-0531
Hours: Mon to Sat 10 a.m. to 7 p.m.
Free

Much more than a bunch of hanging paintings, this gallery features jewelry, pottery, kaleidoscopes, musical instruments, hand blown glass, and books in addition to paintings.

Peter Max Art Gallery
Forum Shops at Caesars Palace
(702) 644-7070
www.petermax.com
Hours: Daily, 10 a.m. to 7 p.m.
Free

Free love followers can flock to the Forum Shops to view and purchase original paintings by the legendary '60s artist Peter Max, known for his psychedelic pop art and images on album covers, race cars, postage stamps, and patriotic murals.

Red Skelton Gallery
7780 South Giles St.
(702) 263-4644
Hours vary, call ahead.
Free

Sin City is home to the world's largest collection of Red Skelton art. Over 1,000 originals, limited edition prints, plaques, sculptures, and plates by the famous Vegas comic are featured.

Symbolic Gallery
4631 Dean Martin Dr.
(702) 507-5263
www.symboliccollection.com
Hours: By appointment, Wed to Sun, noon to 8 p.m.
Free

Music fans will enjoy this gallery's collection of memorabilia, photos, paintings, and jewelry featuring country, rock and roll, and blues artists. The collection also includes rare underground rock art posters, Asian artifacts, original artwork by Von Dutch, rock band photography by Mick Rock, and an exclusive collection of celebrity memorabilia from the life of Bob Dylan and Johnny Cash.

Wyland Galleries of Las Vegas
3667 Las Vegas Blvd. South
(702) 699-5363
www.wylandgalleries.com
Hours vary, call ahead.
Free

Whale and Mickey Mouse admirers won't want to miss this gallery. Resembling an underwater world of whales, sharks, dolphins, sea turtles, and other marine life, this gallery is dedicated to showcasing the works of Wyland, the world's foremost marine life muralist, painter, and sculptor. Also on display are works by Disney artist James Coleman.

FREE **AND** CHEAP **GARDENS**

Who knew anything green could grow in the desert? Just finding your way outside through the eternal smoky twilight of the casinos and their satellite rings of shops can be a challenge. They obviously don't want you out there mooning under the date palms when you could be shedding hundred-dollar bills at the craps tables. Surprisingly, Sin City is home to some fabulous outdoor spaces. Just add water (average annual rainfall here hovers around 4 inches), and you can grow pretty much any tropical or Mediterranean plant. Yes, a lot of it's all themed fantasy, indoors and out, but at least the plants are real. Most of them, anyway.

Bellagio Conservatory
3600 Las Vegas Blvd. South
(702) 693-7111
www.bellagio.com
Daily, 24 hours
Free

Children of nature will love this horticultural heaven. Arched glass ceilings tower 50 feet above the 13,000-square-foot garden, which typically holds 31 trees, 500 shrubs, and 6,000 flowers. Each visit will showcase a new display, as the gardens are totally transformed four times a year, offering guests a guaranteed fresh floral experience on each visit.

Ethel M Cactus Garden
2 Cactus Garden Dr.
(800) 471-0352
www.ethelschocolates.com
Daily, 8:30 a.m. to 6 p.m.
Free

In addition to all that chocolate, the Ethel M Factory houses one of the largest drought-resistant gardens in the country. After getting your cocoa fix at the factory and store, stroll through the four acres of cactus and desert plants with 350 species including eucalyptus, cacti, and succulents. Try to plan your visit around the holidays, when the factory decorates the garden Vegas style with over 100,000 sparkling lights.

Gilcrease Nature Sanctuary and Gardens
8103 Racel St.
(702) 645-4224
www.gilcreasenaturesanctuary.org
Daily, 9 a.m. to 5 p.m.
$5 adults, $1 children

In addition to offering a sanctuary for 1,500 homeless animals including birds, tortoises, turtles, iguanas, goats, pigs, geese, donkeys, and horses, this farm turned animal orphanage also features a butterfly and orchard garden.

Springs Preserve
333 South Valley View Blvd.
(702) 822-7799
www.springspreserve.org
Daily, 10 a.m. to 6 p.m.
$9.95 adults, $4.95 children

This eight-acre preserve houses a huge cactus garden divided into Mojave, Sonoran, Chihuahuan, South American, and Exotica sections, as well as a rose, herb, vegetable, and fruit garden. If you bring your ailing plant on Fridays from 10 a.m. to noon, a plant doctor will provide a free diagnosis and cure.

REAL ESTATE:
BUYING ON THE CHEAP

*"I would give a thousand furlongs of sea
for an acre of barren ground."*

—SHAKESPEARE

The national recession that began in December 2007 continues to grip the nation today, waging an especially brutal war on the construction-based and spending-oriented Las Vegas economy. The money that poured into the city on housing and discretionary dollars propelled Nevada to nation-leading growth in the 1990s and early 2000s, but that formula for expansion couldn't withstand the economic storm that's buffeted the country for the last several years. You know it's bad when they start comparing Nevada to Michigan.

Las Vegas became one of the country's top markets for foreclosures, with approximately 70 percent of Nevada mortgages slipping underwater in 2009 as thousands of bank sales pushed housing prices down toward 2000 averages. If Las Vegas is where you'd like to live (or have a second home), someone else's disaster may be your bargain. Below are some agencies that can provide assistance to help residents get their own affordable piece of Sin City.

HOMES ON THE CHEAP: BUYING IN THE TIME OF FORECLOSURE

Neighborhood Development Division
400 Stewart Ave.
(702) 229-2555
www.lasvegasnevada.gov

Through the city's homebuyer assistance program, potential buyers can borrow up to $10,000 for help with a down payment and closing costs for a home or condo located in the city limits of Las Vegas. They also offer information on grants, educational programs, and help finding city-subsidized real estate.

Nevada Fair Housing Center
3380 West Sahara, Suite 150
(702) 731-6095
www.nfhc.org

Folks at the Nevada Fair Housing Center can provide free advice and classes as well as assistance in qualifying for a loan and purchasing a property for potential homebuyers. They can also help find funds for down payment assistance as well as provide home buyer education information, all for free. Classes are offered in both English and Spanish.

Realtor.com
www.realtor.com

Through Realtor.com, the Web site of the National Association of Realtors, you can view new properties, explore different neighborhoods, check your credit, find local mortgage rates, and calculate potential monthly mortgage payments on properties all from the comfort of your laptop.

Relocating to Las Vegas
www.lvrelocationguide.com

This online resource houses all you need if you're thinking of relocating to Sin City. It includes job postings, apartment and home rentals, information about different neighborhoods, a guide to prepare for home ownership, and lots of other useful info about living in Las Vegas. You can order a free "Relocating to Las Vegas" brochure from the Web site.

WORK **FOR** YOUR **RENT**

You can live rent-free by working in exchange for housing at a number of professions. Wealthy locals are in need of providers of services they either can't or don't want to do themselves including personal assistants, senior companions, nannies, housekeepers, and butlers. Here is a listing of placement agencies that can help you live rent-free.

Angel Care Nanny Agency

1750 North Buffalo Dr., Suite 104
(702) 485-4723
www.angelcareagency.com

Artsy Nannies

P.O. Box 530784
(702) 448-4352
www.artsynannies.com

Maids and More

3514 East Tropicana Ave.
(702) 436-0136

Molly Maid

6018 West Smoke Ranch Rd.
(702) 647-4451

Nannies and Housekeepers USA

3585 East Flamingo Rd., Suite 204
(702) 451-0021
www.nahusa.com

Nanny's and Granny's

(702) 364-4700
www.nanny4u.com

MEDICAL CARE:
CHEAP CHECKUPS

"We should manage our fortunes as we do our health—enjoy it when good, be patient when it is bad, and never apply violent remedies except in an extreme necessity."

—FRANCOIS DE LA ROCHEFOUCAULD

Sin City is no different than anywhere else in the country when it comes to trying to find affordable health care. Good luck. Even if you have insurance it's likely that it isn't covering as much as it did five years ago. The odds aren't in your favor if you gamble on your well-being, but for many Vegas residents health insurance premiums are just too high, insurance companies are refusing to pay for necessary procedures, and limited access to doctors keeps patients from getting the medical care they need. Luckily, Las Vegas does house hospitals and clinics that offer reduced-cost and sometimes even free care.

CHEAP **CLINICS** AND **CENTERS**

Bridger Health Center
310 South 9th St., Suite 110
(702) 220-9932
www.nvhealthcenters.org

Specializing in senior health, family health, immunizations, and preventive health, this center also has a clinic specializing in foot care. They accept Medicare and Medicaid with a sliding fee schedule for low-income patients without insurance.

Durango Dental Group
3140 South Durango Dr.
(702) 362-1856
www.durangodentalgroup.com

Durango Dental focuses on all kinds of dental work and offers a new patient special. For $39, all new patients can receive digital X-rays, a cleaning, and complete exam. They also offer a "my smile" program that provides discounts on complete x-rays, fillings, crowns, and orthodontic work.

Eastern Family Medical and Dental Center
2212 South Eastern Ave.
(702) 735-9334
www.nvhealthcenter.org

This clinic offers services in family medicine, preventive health care, women and children's health and immunizations, prenatal and newborn care, and general health education. They also provide dental care for patients ages five and up. Appointments are strongly recommended. There is a sliding fee schedule for low-income patients without insurance.

Huntridge Teen Clinic

2100 South Maryland Pkwy.
(702) 369-2616
www.hmtridge.org

This clinic provides medical and dental care to uninsured and at-risk adolescents ages 12 to 19 years old who are ineligible or unable to obtain services available through Clark County agencies. Most services are free of charge.

Las Vegas Outreach Clinic

403 West Wilson Ave.
(702) 380-8511

47 West Owens Ave.
(702) 307-4635
www.nvhealthcenter.org

Mostly geared toward homeless people but anyone in need can see a doctor, both clinics offer a variety of services including both physical and mental medical attention. These clinics are entirely free of charge.

MiniCare

Meadows Mall Clinic
3838 Meadows Lane
(702) 220-3838
www.minicare.ning.com

This nonprofit center provides low cost primary care to millions of Americans who cannot afford to see a doctor. Each member pays a $5 annual membership fee and $22 per office visit. MiniCare does not require or accept any form of insurance. MiniCare also provides free prescriptions if you qualify. Check the Web site for details.

Nevada Health Centers Mammogram Van

(877) 581-6266
www.nvhealthcenters.org

This mobile van travels to underserved areas and provides mammograms to geographically isolated or uninsured women. All tests are free of charge. Call for appointments.

Pacific Family Clinic
8440 West Lake Mead Blvd.
(702) 341-9666

This clinic offers a variety of medical services and testing for the general public as well as chiropractor, dietician, and nutritionist services. Appointments are necessary and it is not free, but prices are cheaper than visits at a specialist.

Paradise Park Children's Dental Clinic
4770 Harrison Dr.
(702) 432-3224
www.tinyteeth.org

This nonprofit clinic provides at-risk youth comprehensive dental care services including cleanings, disease management, and restorative treatments. The 9,500-square-foot facility provides low-cost and free services.

Volunteers in Medicine of Southern Nevada
4770 South Henderson Dr.
(702) 967-0530
www.vmsn.org

Made up of volunteer physicians, nurses, medical assistants, lab techs, and pharmacists, this new clinic provides free medical services for those that qualify.

CLINICAL **TRIALS**

With the economy suffering and millions uninsured, the lure of volunteering for medical research is growing. For many patients, clinical trials are a good way to get lab work covered, or medications, or supplies for monitoring cancer, diabetes, or other chronic conditions. In addition to making managing of their conditions more affordable, the research conducted can help to find cures for many diseases.

Payments to participate in clinical trials often are modest—$25 to $75 per visit to cover travel, time, or inconvenience. But the cash can be dwarfed by the value of free medical care—care that could otherwise cost hundreds or thousands of dollars. Here are some sources to find out what clinical trials are being offered in Las Vegas.

American Diabetes Association
www.diabetes.org

Clinical Connection
www.clinicalconnection.com

Clinical Trial Search
www.clinicaltrialsearch.org

Center Watch
www.centerwatch.com

Impact Clinical Trials
630 South Rancho Dr.
(702) 889-0061
www.impactclinicaltrials.com

National Cancer Institute
www.cancer.gov

APPENDIX A:

CHEAP DATES

You're smitten but you're also broke. But even in Sin City you're not out of luck.

If you're not independently wealthy and haven't enjoyed a profitable run at the slots or poker tables recently, there are plenty of inexpensive activities around Las Vegas that can make for a fun date.

All it takes is a bit of imagination. Here are a few ideas.

Eat outdoors

Let's begin with that classic warm-weather date, the picnic. There are plenty of picnic-friendly parks around the valley, ranging from city parks (Lorenzi or Sunset, or take a look at the parks index) and federal lands such as Mount Charleston, all of which offer a chance to dine under an open sky.

You can control the cost of your brunch, dinner, or lunch, which can save some money for the after-eating portion of your date. Check out the selection of cheeses, crackers, smoked seafoods, wine, and other tasty goodies at Costco and Trader Joe's and you'll find you can get away with a gourmet dinner for much less than a trip to a Strip restaurant.

Then comb discount stores such as Target, 99c Stores, or Walgreen's for an inexpensive picnic basket, champagne glasses, and linens and assemble the spread yourself.

Hit the road

A pleasant drive can be romantic, too, but Las Vegas is at least a few hours away from most vacation-type destinations.

Take a trip to romantic Mount Charleston instead. And, when you get there, stop in at the Mount Charleston Lodge for an inexpensive drink and some priceless mountain views.

In wintertime you can enjoy the fireplace for free, snuggle up, and down some hot cocoa or cider, and in the summer you can steal away from the heat on the Strip for some lemonade or spritzers on the patio.

See some stars

You can indulge in some romantic stargazing with your date at the Community College of Southern Nevada's planetarium, 3200 East Cheyenne Ave., in North Las Vegas.

Another way to see stars: take your date on a European vacation; well, sort of. Whisk her to the fake City of Lights via the Eiffel Tower Experience at Paris Las Vegas, 3645 Las Vegas Blvd, South.

At 50 stories, the tower is a half-scale reproduction of the real Eiffel Tower in the real Paris. It boasts an observation deck that provides visitors with a view of the valley, and the stars at night, from 460 feet above the Strip.

Weather permitting, the tower is open daily from 9:30 a.m. to 12:30 a.m. General admission is $9. Okay, that's about $20 for two, but it sure beats two round tickets to Paris.

Get artsy

Nothing impresses a date more than class and culture. Besides, a trip to the Bellagio Gallery of Fine Art, 3600 Las Vegas Blvd. South, offers practical dating benefits, too.

Unlike a trip to a concert, movie, or nightclub, you'll actually be able to talk with your date. After the art, you can wander outside and see the free fountain show.

Have a kitschy time

The Fremont Street Experience gets a bad rap sometimes, but only from people who compare it to someplace such as the Strip.

Our advice: Explain to your date that the Fremont Street Experience actually is a sort of corporate street fair.

Amble among the kiosks and balloon vendors and traveling entertainers. Check out the souvenir stands and cheap eats—that $1.99 shrimp cocktail at the Golden Gate is just made for strolling—and enjoy the occasional free performers and concerts and general party atmosphere.

Then, to give your date a memento of your time together, shell out a few bucks for a caricature from one of those sidewalk artists. Nothing impresses a date like a grotesquely exaggerated portrait.

Grab the deals

There are plenty of good, inexpensive shows around town, although you sometimes might have to plan your date for afternoon or early evening to experience the best value.

Some will only set you back a one-drink minimum, which is still pretty cheap for a date. Check the theater section to find some great free and inexpensive shows.

Smell the flowers

Can't afford roses for your date? After you visit the gallery of fine art, head to the Bellagio's conservatory for more flowers and fauna then anyone could ever afford to buy. Or, take an afternoon date to the Springs Reserve and for under $20 you can stroll through miles of different varieties of gardens. You can also take a hand-in-hand nature walk.

APPENDIX B:

RETRO LAS VEGAS, BABY

What happens in Vegas rarely stays in Vegas. It gets imploded to make way for a new megaresort.

The building boom that began with the Mirage in 1989 has transformed Las Vegas into a city of laser shows, glitzy malls, celebrity-chef restaurants, and high-end gambling.

Sin City has staked much of its reputation on its past, and yet how sinful it is that so little of that past remains.

The Dunes? The Sands? The Hacienda? All of these legendary casinos were eradicated during the Vegas implosion boom of the early-to-mid '90s. It's understandable. Tradition, preservation, and scale are funny things in a city where Paris is but a mile from New York.

But what about the shrimp cocktail, old joints, Rat Pack, neon lights, and sinful spirit that made Vegas famous? They're still here; you just have to look hard to find them.

The search for retro Vegas provides the color and flair that made the city what it is, even if it doesn't look that way these days.

It'll also make you remember your trip long after what you saw has imploded. Because, eventually, it will be. If you're hankering for old style Vegas, here are some stops to get you in the mood.

Shrimp cocktail, anyone? Once a Vegas staple, the shrimp cocktail has almost disappeared along with the joints that used to serve it. Ask for one at the Bellagio and you'll get a strange look or directions to Michael Mina, where a shrimp-based entree fetches around 40 bucks.

Instead, go to the Golden Gate Casino, 1 Fremont St., in downtown Vegas. The 1906 casino is not only the oldest parlor in Vegas, it's also the birthplace of the shrimp cocktail. The $1.99 price tag and old-style look and retro vibe of the joint have made the Golden Gate a Vegas institution.

Bring on the showgirls

Donn Arden ruffled feathers when he hit Vegas. The godfather of the Vegas showgirl, Arden brought the French stage show here, on a grand scale, of course. In 1958, it created a spectacle. Today, it's an institution. Though Arden died in 1994, his show, *Jubilee!*, still goes on at **Bally's Casino,** 3645 Las Vegas Blvd. South.

Yes, the show boasts statuesque showgirls in feathers and sequined skimpiness. But it also features grand-scale stunts only a showman such as Arden could dream of, such as the sinking of the *Titanic* in an ocean of water. You can even take the *Jubilee!* All Access Backstage Walking Tour and get a glimpse of the showgirl life.

Time machine

Every casino has a chic lounge; some have many. But old-school swanky is hard to find. That's why the **Peppermill Fireside Lounge** sticks out like a sharkskin suit. A Vegas institution, the Peppermill, 2985 Las Vegas Blvd. South, has seen a number of makeovers since the early '70s. But it still exudes the kind of retro charm you see only, well, here.

The waitresses wear long black gowns and look as if they just walked out of a Vegas time machine. The walls are covered in mirrors, with glowing light bouncing around the room. It's cozy instead of the usual Las Vegas garishness, especially around the fire pit emanating from a pool of glowing water. It adds up to a moody hot spot for Vegas romantics, in love with the vibe of a bygone era.

Neon glows

Upscale megaresorts frown on neon. It's understandable. The Bellagio and Wynn Las Vegas are too classy. And the Paris and Venetian want to pretend they're, well, Paris and Venice.

And yet, what is Las Vegas without neon? That answer lies at the **Neon Museum,** an outdoor installation of vintage Vegas neon in the downtown Fremont Street district. Most of the signs come from demolished hotels like the Hacienda or Desert Inn.

But it also reflects the neon craze that overtook Vegas in the '50s, so much so that dairies, restaurants, and bowling alleys joined in on the garish fun. The Neon Museum also has a neon boneyard that's open for tours. Check out www.neonmuseum.org.

Big band night

Once upon a time, every casino had its own live orchestra. Then came the

1980s, when the operators busted the musicians' union, the bands, and the concept. The result?

A city rich in old-school players with few spots to play in. That's why, come Friday, they hit **Pogo's Tavern**, 2103 North Decatur Blvd. Big Band Night is a reminder of the rich tradition of music in Vegas even if the only glitz in the bar is the shiny curtain behind the stage.

Liberace lives

Flamboyantly tasteless. Tacky. Ostentatious. Over the top. Yeah, there are about a hundred other words for Mr. Showmanship—none of which connotes a modern image.

All the glitz, glitter, and schmaltz are on display at the **Liberace Museum**, 1775 East Tropicana Ave. Check out Liberace's candelabrum ring. Or his red-white-and-blue hot pants. Or his mirrored Rolls Royce. It makes Elton John seem downright frugal. Go to www.liberace.org.

Spaghetti, anyone?

No, the food isn't cooked by Wolfgang Puck. But that shouldn't keep you from **Battista's Hole in the Wall**, 4041 Audrie St., behind the Flamingo Hilton. The Italian eatery flows with Rat Pack kitsch, from the pictures of old Vegas celebs on the walls to an accordionist who plays "That's Amore."

Gambling hall

The red velvet bordello-like wallpaper and dark mahogany decor screams old-school Vegas, But **Binion's Gambling Hall**, 128 Fremont St., isn't just some kitschy reminder of the past. The joint remains a magnet for cigar-chomping poker buffs, because it played host to the World Series of Poker—but also because it was founded by Benny Binion, who brought the high-roller concept to Vegas. Throw in a coffee shop that serves cheap late-night steak dinners and you have an amusement park where the thrill comes from taking in the vibes that made Vegas famous. Check out www.binions.com.

APPENDIX C:

PAWN SHOPS

Ace Loan Company
215 North 3rd St.
(702) 384-5771

Apache Pawn
4230 North Pecos Rd. # 12
(702) 632-3200

ASAP Auto Pawn
6250 Mountain Vista St.
(702) 451-3800

Bargain Pawn
1901 Las Vegas Blvd. North
(702) 399-9950

Cash America Super Pawn
3252 Las Vegas Blvd. North
(702) 643-9851

300 North Nellis Blvd.
(702) 438-2200

6424 Losee Rd. # 135
(702) 873-5823

Cash Exchange & Money Store
616 Las Vegas Blvd. South
(702) 385-2274

Cash in a Flash
1942 East Sahara Ave.
(702) 313-2274

Desert Inn Pawn
3050 East Desert Inn Rd. # 104
(702) 737-3385

EZ Pawn
212 Las Vegas Blvd. South
(702) 474-7324

808 Las Vegas Blvd. South
(702) 384-3042

1501 East Charleston Blvd.
(702) 383-0988

1832 Las Vegas Blvd. North
(702) 649-8533

821 North Rancho Dr.
(702) 631-7296

3010 South Valley View Blvd.
(702) 385-7711

2820 East Craig Rd.
(702) 632-3200

6032 West Cheyenne Ave.
(702) 385-4292

2200 South Rainbow Blvd.
(702) 870-7296

1241 North Boulder Hwy.
(702) 565-5626

10075 South Eastern Ave. # 111
(702) 384-7296

E-Z Cash Superpawn
2300 East Charleston Blvd.
(702) 477-3040

2645 South Decatur Blvd.
(702) 871-4464

5910 West Lake Mead Blvd.
(702) 438-2123

First Class Pawn and Jewelry
4635 West Flamingo Rd.
(702) 252-7296

Gold Exchange
420 East Sahara Ave.
(702) 997-0361

Gun Place
6250 Mountain Vista Dr. # M1
(702) 450-4867

John's Loan and Jewelry
2230 Paradise Rd.
(702) 383-0744

Max Pawn and Jewelry Superstores
2400 South Jones Blvd. #15
(702) 253-7296

Metro Pawn
2490 North Rancho Dr.
(702) 260-7396

National Jewelry Liquidation
3021 Business Lane
(702) 739-6197

Nevada Title Loan
1810 Las Vegas Blvd. North
(702) 649-5052

Pawn Place
119 North 4th St.
(702) 385-7296

Pawn Place II
2416 Tam Dr.
(702) 385-4292

Pawn Place III
5624 West Charleston Blvd.
(702) 870-7296

Pawn Plus
4401 East Sunset Rd.
(702) 451-5505

2081 West Sunset Rd.
(702) 649-7100

36 West Horizon Ridge Pkwy.
(702) 648-5200

Pawn Shop Management
6859 South Eastern Ave. # 101
(702) 851-8155

Pioneer Loan and Jewelry
111 North 1st St.
(702) 384-2970

520 North Eastern Ave. # 150
(702) 380-8113

Postal Place
117 North 4th St.
(702) 383-3337

Sahara Pawn
2400 South Jones Blvd. # 15
(702) 253-7296

Stoney's
126 South 1st St.
(702) 384-2686

SuperPawn
626 Las Vegas Blvd. South
(702) 382-2486

126 South 1st St.
(702) 384-2686

2645 South Decatur Blvd.
(702) 871-4464

3480 Spring Mountain Rd.
(702) 364-1103

515 East Saint Louis Ave.
(702) 792-2900

6824 West Cheyenne Ave.
(702) 655-4498

300 North Nellis Blvd.
(702) 438-2200

3252 Las Vegas Blvd. North
(702) 643-9851

5716 Boulder Hwy.
(702) 898-2200

5695 Boulder Hwy.
(702) 898-2200

4111 North Rancho Dr.
(702) 438-1543

2300 East Bonanza Rd.
(702) 387-2888

2300 East Charleston Blvd.
(702) 477-3040

3270 South Valley View Blvd.
(702) 382-2486

2020 West Craig Rd. # 200,
(702) 638-0323

3021 Business Lane
(702) 739-6197

4635 West Flamingo Rd.
(702) 302-4828

1150 South Rainbow Blvd.
(702) 318-4900

7585 West Washington Ave.
(702) 302-4301

6424 Losee Rd.
(702) 873-5823

1100 West Sunset Rd.
(702) 302-4211

7095 North Durango Dr.
(702) 777-1011

2646 West Horizon Ridge Pkwy. # A2
(702) 407-8900

Tool Place
5620 West Charleston Blvd.
(702) 878-5626

APPENDIX D:

PARKS

All American Park
Buffalo Drive and Oakey Boulevard

- Dog Run (1)
- Football Fields (5)
- Playgrounds (2)
- Picnic Areas (2)
- Jogging/Walking Track
- Tennis Courts (4)

Aloha Shores Park
Cheyenne Avenue and Buffalo Drive

- Bocce Court
- Horseshoe Courts (2)
- Playground
- Picnic Area
- Tennis Courts (2)
- Roller Hockey Rink
- Volleyball Courts (2)

Angel Park
Westcliff Drive and Durango Drive

- Baseball/Softball Field
- Playground
- Fitness Course
- Jogging/Walking Path
- Picnic Areas (3)
- Tennis Courts (2)

Ansan Sister City Park
Villa Monterey and Ducharme Avenue

- Fitness Course
- Jogging/Walking Path
- Playground
- Picnic Areas (2)
- Tennis Courts (2)
- Volleyball Court
- Soccer Field

Bob Baskin Park
South Rancho Drive and West Oakey Boulevard

- Playground
- Basketball Court
- Picnic Area
- Jogging/Walking Track
- Tennis Courts (4)
- Fitness Course
- Water Play Area

Bruce Trent Park
Vegas Drive and Rampart Boulevard

- Fitness Course
- Playgrounds (2)
- Picnic Areas (8)
- Tennis Courts (2)
- Water Play Area

Centennial Hills Park
Buffalo Drive and Elkhorn Road

- Picnic Areas
- Dog Runs (2)
- Sand Volleyball Courts (10)
- Soccer Fields (2)
- Playgrounds (one is a universal playground with ramps and features for all abilities)
- Water Play Areas (2)
- Jogging/Walking Path with interpretive signage describing the historical significance of the area

Charleston Heights Park
Maverick Street and Smoke Ranch Road

- Basketball Court
- Jogging/Walking Path
- Picnic Areas (6)
- Playgrounds (2)
- Roller Hockey Rink
- Tennis Court

Children's Memorial Park
Gowan Road and Torrey Pines Drive

- Baseball/Softball Fields (6)
- Basketball Courts (2)
- Bocce Courts (2)
- Concession Stand
- Dog Park (2 dog runs)
- Fitness Course
- Horseshoe Courts (2)
- Jogging/Walking Paths (2)
- Playgrounds (4)

- Roller Hockey Rink
- Tennis Courts (2)

Dexter Park
Upland Boulevard north of West Charleston Boulevard

- Baseball/Softball Field
- Playground
- Basketball Courts (2)
- Picnic Areas (5)
- Tennis Courts (2)

Doc Romeo Park
West Cheyenne Avenue and Ronemus Drive

- Baseball/Softball Fields (8)
  60-foot youth baseball fields (2)
  youth softball fields (2)
  multipurpose youth/adult softball fields (3)
  90-foot youth/adult baseball field (1)
- Skate Park
- Playgrounds (2)

Doolittle Park
West Lake Mead Boulevard and J Street

- Baseball/Softball Fields (3)
- Bocce Courts (3)
- Fitness Course
- Jogging/Walking Path
- Horseshoe Courts (2)
- Playground
- Picnic Area

Durango Hills Park

- 18-hole Executive Golf Course
- Basketball Courts (2)
- Skate Park
- Walking/Jogging Track
- Tennis Courts
- Picnic Area
- Playground

Ed Fountain Park
Vegas Drive and Decatur Boulevard

- Baseball/Softball Fields (3)
- Artificial Turf Soccer/Football Fields (2)
- Real Turf Soccer/Football Fields (3)
- Concession Stand
- Basketball Court
- Playground
- Picnic Area

Ethel Pearson Park
West Washington Avenue and D Street

- Basketball Courts (2)
- Jogging/Walking Path
- Playground
- Roller Hockey Rink
- Pavement Games

Freedom Park
850 North Mojave Road

- Baseball/Softball Fields (6)
- Skate Park
- Bocce Courts (2)
- Horseshoe Courts (4)

- Concession Stand
- Fitness Course
- Jogging/Walking Path
- Playgrounds (4)
- Picnic Areas (23)
- Soccer Practice Fields (3)

Garehime Heights Park
Campbell Drive and Alexander Road

- Playgrounds (2)
- Picnic Areas (7)
- Basketball Courts (2)
- Tennis Courts (2)
- Skate Bowl
- Jogging/Walking Path

Gilcrease Brothers Park
Grand Teton and Hualapai Way

- Bocce Courts (2)
- Shuffleboard Courts (2)
- Horseshoe Pits (2)
- Shaded Play Areas
- Walking Path
- Shaded Picnic Areas

Justice Myron E. Leavitt Family Park
East St. Louis Avenue and Eastern Avenue

- Lighted Artificial Turf Soccer Field
- Playgrounds (2)
- Dog Runs (3)
- Bocce Courts (10)
- Fitness Course Equipment
- Horseshoe Courts (6)

- Walking Path
- Shade Structures (3 are reservable)
- Shuffleboard Courts (16)

Lorenzi Park
West Washington Avenue and Twin Lakes Drive

- Sammy Davis Jr. Festival Plaza
- Baseball/Softball Fields (4)
- Basketball Courts (2)
- Concession Stand
- Dog Runs (2)
- Fitness Course
- Jogging/Walking Path
- Playgrounds (3)
- Pond
- Tennis Courts (10)
- Picnic Areas (15)

Mountain Ridge Park
Durango Drive and Elkhorn Road

- Baseball/Softball Fields (7)
- Playground
- Skate Park
- Roller Hockey Rink
- Tennis Courts (2)
- Jogging/Walking Path

Pioneer Park
Braswell Drive and Pioneer Way

- Playgrounds (2)
- Basketball Court
- Picnic Areas (7)
- Bocce Courts (2)
- Horseshoe Courts (3)
- Jogging/Walking Path

Police Memorial Park
Cheyenne Avenue and Metro Academy Way

- Playgrounds (2)
- Dog Park (3 dog runs)
- Basketball Court
- Picnic Area
- Jogging/Walking Path
- Tennis Courts (2)
- Skate Bowl
- Roller Hockey Rink
- Desert Garden
- Fallen Officer Tree Grove and Memorial Wall
- Lou Gehrig's (ALS) Tree Grove

Rafael Rivera Park
28th Street and Stewart Avenue

- Baseball/Softball Field
- Fitness Course
- Horseshoe Court
- Picnic Areas (4)
- Playgrounds (2)
- Soccer Field
- Tennis Court

Stewart Park
Marion Drive south of Stewart

- Playgrounds (2)
- Horseshoe Courts (2)
- Water Play Area
- Jogging/Walking Path
- Basketball Courts (2)
- Tennis Courts (4)
- Fitness Course

Sunny Springs Park
Buffalo Drive and Golden Talon Avenue

- Playgrounds (2)
- Horseshoe Courts (2)
- Water Play Area
- Jogging/Walking Path
- Basketball Courts (2)
- Tennis Courts (4)
- Fitness Course

W. Wayne Bunker Family Park
Tenaya Way and Alexander Road

- Playgrounds (2)
- Soccer Courts (2)
- Picnic Areas (6)
- Tennis Courts (2)
- Jogging/Walking Path
- Skate Park
- Volleyball Court
- Horseshoe Courts (12)

HORSE PARKS

Bradley Bridle Park
Horse and Bradley Road

- Two round pens, one lighted
- One large arena with lights and bleacher seating
- One shaded corral
- Pull-through parking stalls for trailers

- Perimeter trail
- Three shaded picnic areas

DOG PARKS

All American Park
Buffalo Drive and Oakey Boulevard

Barkin' Basin Park
Tenaya and Alexander

- Three separated dog cells
- Shaded seating areas for owners
- Dog and people water fountains

Centennial Hills Park
Buffalo Drive and Elkhorn Road

- Dog Runs (2)

Children's Memorial Park
Gowan Road and Torrey Pines Drive

- Dog Park (2 dog runs)

Justice Myron E. Leavitt Family Park
East St. Louis Avenue and Eastern Avenue

- Dog Runs (3)

Lorenzi Park
West Washington Avenue and Twin Lakes Drive

- Dog Runs (2)

Police Memorial Park

Cheyenne Avenue and Metro Academy
Way

• Dog Park (3 dog runs)

Winding Trails Park

7250 Fort Apache Rd.

• Dog Park

Woofter Park

Rock Springs and Vegas Drive

• Dog Park (2 dog runs)

APPENDIX E:

RECREATION CENTERS

Bunkerville Community Center
150 Virgin St.
(702) 346-5260
Mon to Fri, 8 a.m. to noon

Cambridge Recreation Center
3300 Cambridge St.
(702) 455-7169
Mon to Fri, 7 a.m. to 8 p.m.
Sat, 10 a.m. to 2 p.m.

Cora Coleman Senior Center
2100 Bonnie Lane
(702) 455-7617
Mon to Fri, 7:30 a.m. to 5 p.m.

Desert Breeze Community Center
8275 Spring Mountain Rd.
(702) 455-8334
Mon to Fri, 7 a.m. to 8 p.m.
Sat 9 a.m. to 4 p.m.

Helen Meyer Community Center
4525 New Forest Dr.
(702) 455-7723
Mon to Fri, 7 a.m. to 8 p.m.

Hollywood Recreation and Community Services Center
1650 South Hollywood
(702) 455-0566
Mon to Fri, 6 a.m. to 8 p.m.
Sat, 9 a.m. to 5 p.m.

Indian Springs Recreation Center
715 West Gretta Lane
(702) 879-3890
Mon to Thurs, 9 a.m. to 1 p.m.

Moapa Community Center
1340 East Hwy 168
(702) 864-2423
Mon to Thurs, 8 a.m. to 9 p.m.

Moapa Valley Community Center
320 Whipple Ave.
(702) 398-7480
Mon to Fri, 8 a.m. to 4 p.m.

Mountain Crest Neighborhood Services Center
4701 North Durango Rd.
(702) 455-1905
Mon to Fri, 9 a.m. to 6 p.m.

Paradise Recreation and Community Center
4775 McLeod
(702) 455-7513
Mon to Fri, 7 a.m. to 8 p.m.

Parkdale Community Center
3200 Ferndale St.
(702) 455-7517
Mon to Fri, 7 a.m. to 6 p.m.

Robert Price Recreation Center
2050 Bonnie Lane
(702) 455-7600
Mon to Fri, 8 a.m. to 6 p.m.

Spirit Mountain Activity Center
1975 Arie Ave.
(702) 298-3413
Mon to Fri, 8 a.m. to 4 p.m.

Walnut Recreation Center
3075 North Walnut Rd.
(702) 455-8402
Mon to Fri, 7 a.m. to 8 p.m.
Sat, 10 a.m. to 2 p.m.

West Flamingo Center for Active Adults
6255 West Flamingo
(702) 455-7742
Mon to Fri, 8 a.m. to 5:30 p.m.

Whitney Senior Center
5712 East Missouri
(702) 455-7560
Mon to Fri, 9 a.m. to 4 p.m.

Winchester Cultural Center
3130 South McLeod
(702) 455-7340
Tues to Fri, 10 a.m. to 8 p.m.
Sat and Sun, 9 a.m. to 8 p.m.

APPENDIX F:

PUBLIC GOLF COURSES

Angel Park Golf Club
100 South Rampart Blvd.
(888) 446-5358
Cloud Nine Course
9 holes over 1,465 yards with a par of 36

Angel Park Golf Club
100 South Rampart Blvd.
(888) 446-5358
Mountain Course
18 holes over 6,722 yards with a par of 71

Palm Course
18 holes over 6,530 yards with a par of 70

Anthem Country Club
1 Club Side Dr.
(702) 614-5050
Anthem Course
18 holes over 7,267 yards with a par of 72

Bali Hai Golf Course
5160 Las Vegas Blvd. South
(888) 427-6682
Bali Hai Course
18 holes over 6,994 yards with a par of 71

Bear's Best Las Vegas Golf Club
11111 West Flamingo Rd.
(702) 804-8500
Bear's Best Course
18 holes over 7,229 yards with a par of 72

Callaway Golf Center
6730 Las Vegas Blvd. South
(702) 896-4100 ext. 7320
Divine Nine Course
9 holes over 1,230 yards with a par of 27

Desert Pines Golf Club
3415 East Bonanza Rd.
(702) 388-4400 ext. 2
Desert Pines Course
18 holes over 6,810 yards with a par of 71

Desert Rose Golf Course
5483 Club House Dr.
(702) 431-4653
Desert Rose Course
18 holes over 6,511 yards with a par of 71

Desert Willow Golf Course
2020 West Horizon Ridge Pkwy.
(702) 263-4653
Desert Willow Course
18 holes over 3,811 yards with a par
of 60

Durango Hills Golf Club
3501 North Durango Dr.
(702) 229-4653
Durango Course
18 holes over 3,800 yards with a par
of 58

Eagle Crest Golf Club
2203 Thomas W. Ryan Blvd.
(702) 240-1320 ext. 3
Eagle Crest Course
18 holes over 4,067 yards with a par
of 60

The Falls Golf Club
101 Via Vin Santo
(702) 740-5258
The Falls Course
18 holes over 7,250 yards with a par
of 72

Highland Falls Golf Club
10201 Sun City Blvd.
(800) 803-0758
Highland Falls Course
18 holes over 6,512 yards with a par
of 72

Las Vegas Golf Club
4300 West Washington Ave.
(702) 646-3003
Las Vegas Course
18 holes over 6,631 yards with a par
of 72

Las Vegas National Golf Club
1911 East Desert Inn Rd.
(800) 468-7918
Las Vegas National Course
18 holes over 6,815 yards with a par
of 71

The Legacy Golf Club
130 Par Excellence Dr.
(888) 446-5358
Legacy Course
18 holes over 7,233 yards with a par
of 72

Los Prados Golf Course
5150 Los Prados Circle
(702) 645-5696
Los Prados Course
18 holes over 5,348 yards with a par
of 70

Painted Desert Golf Club
5555 Painted Mirage Rd.
(702) 645-2570
Painted Desert Course
18 holes over 6,840 yards with a par
of 72

Palm Valley Golf Course
9201 del Webb Blvd.
(800) 803-0758
Palm Valley Course
18 holes over 6,849 yards with a par
of 72

Red Rock Country Club
2250A Red Springs Dr.
(866) 943-4653
Arroyo Course
18 holes over 6,883 yards with a par
of 72

Mountain Course
18 holes over 6,965 yards with a par
of 72

Revere Golf Club
2600 Hampton Rd.
(877) 273-8373
Concord Course
18 holes over 7,034 yards with a par
of 72

Lexington Course
18 holes over 7,143 yards with a par
of 72

Rhodes Ranch Golf Club
20 Rhodes Ranch Pkwy.
(888) 311-8337
Rhodes Ranch Course
18 holes over 6,800 yards with a par
of 72

Royal Links Golf Club
5995 Vegas Valley Dr.
(888) 427-6682
Royal Links Course
18 holes over 7,029 yards with a par
of 72

Siena Golf Club
10575 Siena Monte Ave.
(888) 689-6469
Siena Course
18 holes over 6,816 yards with a par
of 72

Silverstone Golf Club
8600 Cupp Dr.
(877) 888-2127
Desert Course
9 holes over 3,560 yards with a par
of 36

Mountain Course
9 holes over 3,599 yards with a par
of 36

Valley Course
9 holes over 3,398 yards with a par
of 36

TPC Las Vegas
9851 Canyon Run Dr.
(888) 321-5701
TPC Las Vegas Course
18 holes over 6,772 yards with a par
of 71

Tuscany Golf Club
901 Olivia Pkwy.
(866) 887-2269
Tuscany Course
18 holes over 6,906 yards with a par
of 72

WildHorse Golf Club
2100 West Warm Springs Rd.
(702) 434-9000
WildHorse Course
18 holes over 7,053 yards with a par
of 72

INDEX

ABOUT THE AUTHOR

Shaena Engle is a food and travel writer and president of Engle Communications, a Los Angeles based public relations firm. Her Web site, www.thedivinedish.com, includes reviews of hotels and restaurants and interviews with top chefs and other interesting people. She was destined to become a cheap bastard when her love of travel and food collided with the reality of living on a writer's salary.

She is a freelance writer for a variety of publications, including the *Los Angeles Times, Pasadena* magazine, www.lowfares.com, and *PokerPro* magazine. She has authored two books, *The Best Places to Kiss in Southern California* (a romantic travel guide) and *Silver Linings: Triumphs of The Chronically Ill and Physically Challenged*. Shaena has also authored several iPhone applications, including "The Best Places to Kiss in LA," "The Best Places to Kiss in Las Vegas," "Food Lovers Guide to Las Vegas" and "The Best Places to Kiss in Palm Springs." She is also an amateur magician and often writes on gambling, poker, and magical happenings.